THE SOUP COOKBOOK

Turn Everyday Ingredients into Gourmet Bowls with Simple Recipes to
Satisfy Any Occasion and Every Diet

Nora J. Shepherd

For Nonna Lucia, whose love and simple ingredients turned every meal into a cherished memory. Thank you for showing me the magic of a well-made soup.

TABLE OF CONTENTS

FREE SUPPLEMENTARY RESOURCES

Get ready to elevate your soup-making skills and create bowls of goodness that are as delicious as they are nutritious! To ensure you're fully equipped to master every recipe in this cookbook, we've compiled an array of valuable resources. These tools are designed to help you create stunning soups, from garnishing techniques to healthy options, and take your soup experience to the next level.

Here's what you'll find:

- A Soup Garnishing Guide: Discover how to add the perfect finishing touch to every bowl, with tips on using fresh herbs, creative toppings, and techniques that enhance both flavor and presentation.

- A Soup Pairing Guide: Learn the best side dishes, breads, and beverages to complement your soups and create a well-rounded, balanced meal.

- Grandma's Best Soup Recipes to Strengthen Your Health: Grandma knew the secret to boosting health through hearty, homemade soups. Now, I'm sharing her best recipes to keep you strong and nourished.

- No-Cook Summer Delights: Stay cool with light, refreshing soups that don't require any cooking—perfect for those hot summer days.

- Soup Maker's Marvels: Unlock the full potential of your soup maker with expert tips and foolproof recipes for smooth, perfectly blended soups.

Pressure Cooker Presto: Master quick, flavorful soups with pressure cooker techniques that deliver bold tastes in no time.

- Slow Cooker Magic: Create rich, deeply flavored soups with minimal effort using the slow cooker.

Scan the QR code at the end of this book to access your FREE supplementary resources and unlock +100 additional recipes!

TOGETHER WE CREATE

Why Your Support Is Crucial?

Embarking on the creation of this soup cookbook has been one of the most challenging yet rewarding journeys I've ever undertaken. Choosing to bypass traditional publishing, I embraced the role of an independent author, fully dedicated to sharing my passion for soups and helping others create delicious, nutritious meals. It hasn't been easy, but my commitment to providing you with valuable, creative recipes and resources kept me motivated.

This is why your feedback on Amazon is so crucial. Your insights and opinions are not only valuable to me but are essential in helping others discover this book. Here's how you can contribute:

1. If you haven't already, scan the QR code at the end of the book to download FREE supplementary resources.

2. Leave your feedback on Amazon!

To make a greater impact, consider making a brief video to share your thoughts on the book. Alternatively, leaving a review and including a few photos would also be wonderful! Please remember, there's no obligation, but your feedback would be greatly appreciated.

I'm so excited to be on this journey with you. Are you ready to dive into the world of soups and create something delicious? Enjoy every bowl!

WELCOME TO THE SOUP COOKBOOK

Welcome to The Soup Cookbook, where every bowl tells a story, and every recipe is crafted with heart. I'm Nora J. Shepherd, and for as long as I can remember, soups have been a source of comfort, creativity, and nourishment in my life. From humble beginnings in my grandmother's kitchen, where I learned how a few simple ingredients could transform into something magical, I've carried that same passion for soup-making into my own kitchen—and now into yours.

Growing up, I watched my grandmother use whatever ingredients she had on hand—often fresh from her garden or pantry—to create soups that felt like a warm hug. She didn't follow strict recipes; instead, she cooked from the heart, adapting to what was available and always ensuring that nothing went to waste. I've taken that approach and infused it with the flavors I've discovered throughout my life—whether it's the smoky richness of a hearty winter stew, the bright zing of a summer gazpacho, or the comfort of a slow-simmered chicken broth.

This cookbook reflects my belief that **soup is for everyone, no matter your taste, dietary preferences, or cooking skill.** Whether you're cooking for a cozy night in or preparing a meal to impress guests, soups can be simple, elegant, and incredibly satisfying. I've designed these recipes to be accessible, whether you're a seasoned cook or just starting out, with options for every diet.

In The Soup Cookbook, you'll find a collection of my favorite recipes, ranging from classic comfort soups to gourmet bowls that are perfect for any occasion. You'll learn how to turn everyday ingredients into something truly special, with recipes that are as easy to prepare as they are delicious.

Soup has the unique power to bring people together, to warm the soul, and to nourish the body. It's a universal dish, one that crosses cultures, diets, and seasons. I'm thrilled to share my journey with you and hope this cookbook helps you fall in love with soup the way I have. Let's get cooking—one delicious bowl at a time.

With love,

Nora J. Shepherd

PART I: SOUP-MAKING FUNDAMENTALS

At its core, soup is simple—a blend of flavors, textures, and aromas that can be created with as few or as many ingredients as you wish. But there's an art to elevating a simple broth into something that feels gourmet. In this chapter, I'll teach you the essential techniques and strategies you need to consistently create soups that surprise and delight.

The Building Blocks of Great Soup

"Every great soup starts with one simple concept: balance. Whether you're making a quick weeknight dinner or preparing a show-stopping dish for guests, knowing how to balance flavors and textures is what will separate your soup from the ordinary."

Essential Ingredients: What Every Soup Needs

"Great soup doesn't demand exotic ingredients—it relies on everyday staples used thoughtfully. The right balance of broth, vegetables, proteins, and seasoning turns your soup into a canvas of endless possibilities."

- **Base Ingredients:** Water works, but broth builds. The depth of flavor you achieve with a homemade or store-bought broth is unmatched. If you don't have time to make your own, enhance store-bought broth with a splash of soy sauce, a dash of vinegar, or a sprig of fresh herbs. Broth is the backbone of your soup. It's not just about adding liquid—it's about infusing your soup with layers of flavor right from the start. Whether you're going plant-based or making a traditional chicken stock, there are easy ways to enhance store-bought broths or create your own from scratch.

Practical TIPS:

- Vegetable Broth: For a richer flavor, roast your vegetables before simmering them for broth. Roasting enhances sweetness and adds depth to the broth.

- Chicken Stock: A great chicken stock comes from patience—simmering the bones for hours extracts the collagen and gives the broth its velvety texture.

- Bone Broth: For maximum nutrients, add a tablespoon of apple cider vinegar when simmering bones. This helps extract the minerals and gives the broth extra body.

- **Aromatics:** Sautéing onions, garlic, celery, and carrots before adding liquid is non-negotiable for rich, complex flavors. These ingredients form the 'holy trinity' of soup-making—don't skip this step if you want depth in every spoonful.

- Grains & Starches: Potatoes, rice, or noodles provide texture, but don't be afraid to swap in alternatives like quinoa or farro for added nutrition and flavor.

Timing: When to Add Ingredients

"Timing is crucial in soup-making. Adding ingredients in the right order ensures that your vegetables remain tender but not mushy, your proteins stay juicy, and your grains hold their texture."

- **Vegetables:** Root vegetables like potatoes and carrots take longer to cook, so add them at the beginning of your simmer. Quick-cooking vegetables like zucchini or peas should go in at the end to avoid turning to mush.

- **Proteins:** If you're using delicate proteins like fish or shrimp, wait until the last 10 minutes of cooking to add them so they don't overcook.

- **Grains & Pasta:** Cook pasta or rice separately and add it to the soup just before serving to keep it from absorbing too much broth and turning soggy.

Techniques to Elevate Flavor

"Great soups aren't just thrown together; they're built carefully, layer by layer. With a few professional techniques you can extract maximum flavor from simple ingredients, transforming basic soups into gourmet dishes."

- **Sautéing Aromatics:** Take the time to sweat your onions and garlic—don't rush this step. It sets the stage for the rest of your flavors to shine. Low and slow for five minutes will coax out the natural sweetness of these ingredients.

- **Deglazing:** After sautéing, deglaze the pot with wine, vinegar, or broth. This simple technique lifts those flavorful caramelized bits from the bottom, adding complexity to your soup.

- **Simmering vs. Boiling: Remember:** simmer, don't boil. A gentle simmer allows the flavors to meld and prevents delicate ingredients like fish or soft vegetables from breaking apart.

Balancing Flavors: The Key to Great Soup

" A soup can have the best ingredients, but without balance, it falls flat. The key to a memorable bowl of soup lies in achieving a harmony of flavors—salt, sweetness, acidity, and umami—that keeps your taste buds engaged with every bite. Mastering the art of balancing flavors will elevate even the simplest soups into gourmet experiences."

The Four Flavor Pillars

1. **Salty**

- **Why It's Important:** Salt enhances all other flavors in your soup. It helps draw out the natural sweetness in vegetables, the savoriness in meats, and the depth in broths.

- **How to Use It:** Add salt gradually throughout the cooking process, not just at the end. This allows the flavors to build more naturally. Be cautious when using pre-made broths as they often contain salt—taste before adding more.

- **Pro Tip:** Season in layers. Start with a little salt when sautéing aromatics, then adjust after adding your liquids, and taste again right before serving.

2. **Sweetness**

- **Why It's Important:** Sweetness can balance out bitter or acidic flavors, adding warmth and depth to your soup. Sweet doesn't always mean adding sugar—many ingredients naturally bring sweetness to the table.

- **How to Use It:** Carrots, caramelized onions, sweet potatoes, and butternut squash naturally add sweetness. A touch of honey or maple syrup can also soften acidity or round out strong flavors in tomato-based or spicy soups.

- **Pro Tip:** Caramelizing your vegetables, especially onions, is one of the best ways to naturally develop sweetness without adding any extra sugar

3. **Acidity**

- **Why It's Important:** Acidity brightens flavors and cuts through richness. It's the secret weapon for bringing balance to creamy, heavy, or earthy soups, giving them a fresh, clean finish.

- **How to Use It:** Acids come in many forms—lemon juice, vinegar, tomatoes, or even yogurt. Add a squeeze of lemon or a splash of vinegar at the end of cooking to instantly lift the flavors of a soup that feels too heavy or flat.

- **Pro Tip:** When you feel like your soup is missing something but can't put your finger on it, it's often acid that's lacking. A quick splash of lemon juice, vinegar, or even lime can bring everything into focus.

4. **Umami**

- **Why It's Important:** Umami is the savory, deeply satisfying taste that makes soups rich and hearty. It's often described as the "fifth taste" and is responsible for the mouthwatering depth found in broths, mushrooms, soy sauce, and meats.

- **How to Use It:** Ingredients like mushrooms, soy sauce, miso paste, tomato paste, nutritional yeast, and parmesan cheese all deliver umami. Use these ingredients to add depth, especially to vegetarian or vegan soups that might lack the inherent savoriness of meat-based broths.

- **Pro Tip:** For an instant umami boost, stir in a spoonful of miso paste or soy sauce toward the end of cooking. It'll add a salty, savory kick without overwhelming other flavors.

Cooking Methods: Stovetop, Pressure Cooker, Slow Cooker, and Soup Maker

While many soup recipes traditionally start on the stovetop, there are a variety of ways to prepare a delicious soup depending on your schedule and the kitchen appliances you have available. Each method brings its own advantages—whether you're pressed for time or want to let your soup develop deep flavors throughout the day. Understanding how to adapt a recipe across different cooking methods is key to mastering soup-making with versatility.

Stovetop: The Traditional Method

Most soup recipes are designed with stovetop cooking in mind. This method gives you the most control over the cooking process, allowing you to adjust the heat as needed and see your soup develop in real-time.

- **How It Works:** Start by sautéing aromatics (onions, garlic, carrots, etc.) over medium heat. Add liquids, simmer, and cook until ingredients are tender. This method is great for soups that need gradual flavor development and ingredient layering.

- **Best For:** Everyday soups, broth-based soups, and quick dinners.

Pressure Cooker: Speed Without Sacrificing Flavor

The pressure cooker is a game-changer when it comes to making soups quickly, without sacrificing depth of flavor. By cooking ingredients under high pressure, you can achieve results in a fraction of the time. What usually takes hours on the stovetop can be done in 20-30 minutes.

- **How It Works:** After sautéing your aromatics in the pressure cooker's sauté mode, lock the lid, add your broth and ingredients, and cook under pressure. The high heat and pressure rapidly break down tough ingredients (like beans or meat) while sealing in flavors.

- **Best For:** Hearty stews, legume-based soups (lentils, beans), or soups that traditionally require long simmering times (like beef stew or split pea soup).

<u>Adapting Stovetop Soup Recipes to a Pressure Cooker</u>

- Reduce cook time. What would take 1-2 hours on the stovetop can be reduced to 10-30 minutes under pressure.

- Add less liquid. Pressure cookers don't allow for much evaporation, so reduce the amount of broth by about 1/4.

- Add delicate ingredients last. If your soup has delicate vegetables (like spinach or peas), add them after releasing pressure, using the sauté mode to simmer them for 2-3 minutes.

Slow Cooker: Hands-Off Cooking for Deep, Rich Flavors

The slow cooker is perfect when you want to let a soup slowly develop flavors throughout the day without having to monitor it. Simply throw your ingredients in, set it, and let it simmer away. The low, steady heat allows the ingredients to mingle and deepen over time.

- **How It Works:** Add all your ingredients to the slow cooker, set it on low (for 6-8 hours) or high (for 3-4 hours), and walk away. The slow, even heat is ideal for bringing out the natural sweetness in root vegetables and breaking down tougher cuts of meat.

- **Best For:** Bean soups, stews, and soups with root vegetables or tougher cuts of meat.

Adapting Stovetop Soup Recipes to a Slow Cooker

- Extend cooking time. What would take 30-45 minutes on the stovetop should cook for 6-8 hours on low in the slow cooker, or 3-4 hours on high.

- Sauté aromatics first. To build flavor, sauté onions, garlic, and spices before adding them to the slow cooker.

- Layer ingredients. Start with hard vegetables (carrots, potatoes) at the bottom, proteins in the middle, and delicate veggies (like greens) on top. Add delicate ingredients like pasta, spinach, or fresh herbs in the last 30 minutes of cooking.

Soup Maker: Convenience with Consistency

The soup maker takes all the guesswork out of cooking by combining cooking, blending, and temperature control in one appliance. You simply add your ingredients, press a button, and the soup maker does the rest. It's perfect for those who want a hands-off approach with consistently great results.

- **How It Works:** Add prepped ingredients (chopped vegetables, broth, seasonings) to the soup maker and select your desired setting (smooth, chunky, etc.). The soup maker will cook and blend everything to the perfect texture.

- **Best For:** Pureed soups, creamy soups, and smooth vegetable soups.

Adapting Stovetop Soup Recipes to a Soup Maker

- Cut ingredients smaller. Soup makers have a smaller capacity and rely on even cooking, so chopping ingredients uniformly is key.

- Reduce cook time. Since soup makers cook and blend at the same time, they usually take 20-30 minutes, which is much shorter than stovetop simmering.

- Avoid very thick soups. If adapting a stew or thick soup, add extra broth to prevent the soup maker from struggling with blending.

Adapting Recipes Across Cooking Methods

No matter which appliance you use, you can adapt almost any soup recipe to fit your method of choice. The key is understanding how each method handles time, liquid levels, and ingredient textures.

- **Time Adjustment:** Stovetop recipes generally require the most active cooking time, while slow cookers require much longer cook times. Pressure cookers drastically reduce time, while soup makers fall somewhere in the middle.

- **Liquid Levels:** Pressure cookers and soup makers trap moisture, so use less broth or water when adapting these recipes. Slow cookers, on the other hand, can handle a bit more liquid.

- **Ingredient Order:** In a slow cooker, layer your ingredients based on cooking times. In a pressure cooker or soup maker, add everything at once, but consider delicate ingredients separately (added later for best results).

- **Texture Considerations:** For creamy or pureed soups, a soup maker or blender will produce the smoothest results, while a stovetop or slow cooker will retain more texture. Pressure cookers will quickly break down ingredients for a softer texture overall.

Mastering different soup-making methods gives you the ultimate flexibility in the kitchen. Whether you have 30 minutes or 8 hours, there's always a way to get a delicious bowl of soup on the table. Don't be afraid to adapt a recipe to the tool you have—soup is forgiving, and you can achieve rich, flavorful results no matter the method.

Final Thoughts

"If you're short on time, go for the pressure cooker. If you want to let the soup simmer while you go about your day, choose the slow cooker. For pureed perfection, the soup maker has your back. And if you want the hands-on, classic approach, the stovetop is always a reliable choice."

Preserving Soups and Broths
Refrigeration

Refrigeration is ideal for short-term storage, preserving the freshness and flavor of your soup without affecting its texture or taste. For best results, refrigerate soups in smaller portions to make reheating quicker and more convenient.

- **Best for:** Short-term storage (up to 4-5 days)

- **Instructions:**

1. Let the soup or broth cool to room temperature after cooking.

2. Transfer it to airtight containers or mason jars.

3. Label the container with the date of preparation.

4. Store in the refrigerator for up to 4-5 days.

- **Tips:**

  ◦ If you're storing soups with cream or dairy, consume them within 3 days, as these ingredients spoil faster.

○ When storing soups that contain delicate vegetables or pasta, consider separating those ingredients and adding them back in when reheating. This prevents them from becoming overly soft or soggy

Freezing

Freezing is a fantastic method for preserving soups and broths for long-term storage. However, it's essential to understand that some ingredients freeze better than others. While pureed soups and broth-based soups hold up well, dairy and potato-based soups can separate or change texture.

- **Best for:** Long-term storage (up to 3 months or more)

- **Instructions:**

1. Cool the soup or broth to room temperature.

2. Use freezer-safe containers, zip-top bags, or silicone molds. Leave some room at the top (about 1 inch) for expansion during freezing.

3. For liquids like broth, you can freeze them in ice cube trays first, then transfer to a freezer bag for easy portioning.

4. Label with the name and date.

5. Freeze for up to 3 months. Some soups (like pureed vegetable soups or broth-based soups) can last up to 6 months.

- **Tips:**

○ Always freeze in portions that match your typical serving size. This not only speeds up the thawing process but also reduces waste since you'll only thaw what you need.

○ Avoid freezing soups with cream, dairy, or potatoes, as they can separate or become grainy. Instead, add these ingredients when reheating.

○ If you're freezing soups with herbs like cilantro or parsley, add them fresh after reheating to maintain their vibrant flavor and color. Herbs tend to lose their potency after freezing

Canning

Canning soups and broths is the ultimate method for long-term preservation, allowing you to store soups for up to a year. Pressure canning is the safest option for low-acid soups, as it prevents bacterial growth and ensures food safety.

- **Best for:** Long-term storage (up to 1 year)

- **Instructions for Pressure Canning (best for broth and low-acid soups):**

1. Prepare the soup or broth and let it cool slightly.

2. Sterilize mason jars and lids by boiling them for 10 minutes.

3. Fill the jars, leaving 1 inch of headspace at the top.

4. Wipe the rims of the jars, apply the lids, and screw on the bands until finger-tight.

5. Process the jars in a pressure canner according to your canner's instructions. Broths typically need to be processed for 20-25 minutes, depending on the jar size and altitude.

6. Once processed, let the jars cool and check that the lids have sealed (the center of the lid should not pop up when pressed).

7. Label the jars with the date and store them in a cool, dark place for up to 1 year.

- **Tips:**

  ○ While canning may seem daunting, once mastered, it's an efficient way to batch-cook your favorite soups. Just make sure to always follow safe canning practices, such as adjusting for altitude and ensuring jars are sealed properly

  ○ Canning can alter the texture of some ingredients, particularly pasta, rice, and certain vegetables. It's better to add these ingredients fresh when reheating the soup to maintain the desired texture.

General Tips for Preserving Soups and Broths

No matter which method you choose, properly storing soups and broths not only preserves their flavor and quality but also ensures food safety. Taking a few simple steps—like cooling before storing and labeling with dates—can prevent common storage issues, such as bacterial growth or freezer burn.

- **Cool first:** Always let soups and broths cool before storing to avoid condensation and potential bacterial growth.

- **Portion control:** Freeze or refrigerate soups in portion-sized containers to make reheating easier and quicker. If you find yourself making large batches of soup regularly, investing in freezer-safe silicone molds or stackable containers can save space and make portioning easier. These containers are reusable and eco-friendly, making them a smart addition to your kitchen

- **Labeling:** Always label your containers with the contents and date of preparation. It's easy to forget when you made a batch, and this step ensures you're consuming the soup while it's still at its best.

Thawing and Reheating

Properly thawing and reheating frozen soups is crucial for maintaining both safety and flavor.

- Thawing overnight in the refrigerator is the safest method, but if you're in a rush, defrosting in the microwave or under warm water can work, too.

- When reheating, always bring your soup to a boil if it contains meat or dairy. This ensures that it reaches the proper temperature to kill any potential bacteria that may have developed during storage.

- If a soup has thickened too much after freezing, simply add a splash of broth or water while reheating to adjust the consistency. This is particularly useful for pureed soups or those with grains that tend to absorb liquid during storage.

- Reheat soups and broths on the stove or in the microwave until they are fully hot (165°F or 74°C) to ensure food safety.

HOMEMADE BROTHS AND STOCKS

Creating your own broths and stocks at home is a simple yet powerful way to elevate the flavor and nutritional value of your soups, stews, and sauces. Whether you're simmering a light vegetable broth or a deeply rich beef stock, homemade versions pack far more flavor and complexity than store-bought alternatives. With just a few basic ingredients and some time, you can craft broths that serve as the flavorful foundation for countless dishes. From quick fish stocks to nutrient-dense bone broths, these recipes will guide you through the process of making versatile, flavorful bases for all your cooking needs.

CLASSIC VEGETABLE BROTH

Vegan, Gluten-Free,
-Free, Low Sodium, Diabetic Friendly

Servings	Preparation Time	Cooking Time
8	10 minutes	45 minutes

YOU WILL NEED:

- 2 tablespoons olive oil
- 2 medium onions, chopped
- 4 cloves garlic, smashed
- 2 large carrots, chopped
- 2 stalks celery, chopped
- 1 large tomato, chopped
- 1 bay leaf
- 6 sprigs fresh parsley
- 1 teaspoon fine sea salt
- 10 cups (2400 milliliters) water

METHOD:

1. **Start the base:** Heat olive oil in a large pot over medium heat. Add onions, garlic, carrots, and celery. Sauté for about 5 minutes until softened.

2. **Build the flavors:** Add the tomato, bay leaf, parsley, and salt. Stir the vegetables to combine the flavors and cook for another 2 minutes.

3. **Simmer the Broth:** Pour in the water, bring to a boil, then reduce the heat to low. Let it simmer gently for 45 minutes, allowing all the flavors to infuse.

4. **Strain and Serve:** Once cooked, strain the broth through a fine-mesh sieve, discarding the vegetables and herbs. Your broth is ready to use or store.

Nutritional information per serving: 30 calories, 0.5 grams fat, 7 grams carbohydrates, 1.5 grams fiber, 2 grams protein

Expert TIP: This broth freezes well. Store it in an airtight container for up to 3 months.

CHICKEN STOCK

Low Sodium, Gluten-Free

Servings	Preparation Time	Cooking Time
6	15 minutes	2 minutes

YOU WILL NEED:

- 1 whole chicken carcass or 2 pounds (900 grams) chicken bones
- 1 large onion, quartered
- 2 carrots, roughly chopped
- 2 stalks celery, roughly chopped
- 1 bay leaf
- 1 teaspoon black peppercorns
- 10 cups (2400 milliliters) water

METHOD:

1. **Prepare the stock base:** Place the chicken carcass or bones in a large stockpot. Add the onion, carrots, celery, bay leaf, and peppercorns.

2. **Simmer gently:** Pour the water over the ingredients, bring to a boil, then lower the heat to a gentle simmer. Let it cook for 2 hours, occasionally skimming off any foam.

3. **Strain the stock:** Once done, strain the stock through a sieve, discarding the solids. Let the stock cool before storing.

Nutritional information per serving: 40 calories, 1.5 grams fat, 3 grams carbohydrates, 2 grams protein

Expert TIP: Chicken stock can be frozen in ice cube trays, allowing easy portion control when you need small amounts.

BEEF BONE BROTH

Badges: Gluten-Free, Diabetic Friendly, Low Sodium

Servings	Preparation Time	Cooking Time
10	15 minutes	8 hours

YOU WILL NEED:

- 2 pounds (900 grams) beef bones
- 1 medium onion, halved
- 2 carrots, roughly chopped
- 2 stalks celery, roughly chopped
- 4 cloves garlic, smashed
- 2 tablespoons apple cider vinegar
- 10 cups (2400 milliliters) water
- 1 bay leaf

METHOD:

1. **Roast the bones:** Preheat your oven to 400°F (200°C). Place the beef bones on a baking sheet and roast for 30 minutes until deeply browned.

2. **Simmer the Broth:** Transfer the bones to a large pot. Add the onion, carrots, celery, garlic, apple cider vinegar, and bay leaf. Pour the water over, bring to a boil, then reduce to a very low simmer for 8 hours.

3. **Strain and store:** Strain the broth through a sieve and discard the bones and vegetables. Let it cool before storing.

Nutritional information per serving: 50 calories, 2 grams fat, 0 grams carbohydrates, 7 grams protein

Expert TIP: Add apple cider vinegar to extract more minerals from the bones, boosting the nutritional value.

MUSHROOM BROTH

Badges: Vegan, Gluten-Free, Diabetic Friendly, Low Sodium

Servings	Preparation Time	Cooking Time
6	10 minutes	40 minutes

YOU WILL NEED:

- 2 tablespoons olive oil
- 2 cups (200 grams) mixed mushrooms, sliced
- 1 onion, chopped
- 2 cloves garlic, minced
- 1 teaspoon dried thyme
- 1 bay leaf
- 8 cups (1920 milliliters) water

METHOD:

1. **Sauté the Vegetables:** Heat olive oil in a large pot. Add mushrooms, onions, and garlic. Sauté for about 10 minutes until the mushrooms release their liquid and are softened.

2. **Simmer with herbs:** Add the thyme, bay leaf, and water. Bring to a boil, then lower the heat to simmer for 30 minutes.

3. **Strain and enjoy:** Strain the broth, discarding the solids. Serve hot or store for later.

Nutritional information per serving: 20 calories, 1 gram fat, 3 grams carbohydrates, 1 gram protein

Expert TIP: This earthy broth is perfect for enhancing risottos, soups, or sauces.

FISH STOCK

Badges: Gluten-Free, Dairy-Free, Low Sodium

Servings
8

Preparation Time
10 minutes

Cooking Time
1 hour

YOU WILL NEED:

- 2 pounds (900 grams) fish bones and heads
- 1 onion, quartered
- 2 carrots, chopped
- 2 celery stalks, chopped
- 4 cloves garlic, smashed
- 1 bay leaf
- 10 cups (2400 milliliters) water

METHOD:

1. **Start the stock:** Place fish bones and heads into a large stockpot. Add onion, carrots, celery, garlic, bay leaf, and water.
2. **Simmer and skim:** Bring to a boil, then reduce heat and simmer for 1 hour. Skim off any foam that rises to the top.
3. **Strain and cool:** Strain through a fine sieve and let cool before storing.

Nutritional information per serving: 30 calories, 0.5 grams fat, 4 grams carbohydrates, 3 grams protein

Expert TIP: Use fresh fish bones from non-oily fish like cod or haddock for a cleaner taste.

TURKEY STOCK

Badges: Low Sodium, Diabetic Friendly

Servings
8

Preparation Time
15 minutes

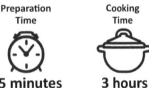
Cooking Time
3 hours

YOU WILL NEED:

- 1 turkey carcass (about 2 pounds or 900 grams)
- 1 large onion, quartered
- 3 carrots, chopped
- 3 celery stalks, chopped
- 1 bay leaf
- 1 teaspoon black peppercorns
- 12 cups (2880 milliliters) water

METHOD:

1. **Prepare the stockpot:** Add the turkey carcass, onion, carrots, celery, bay leaf, and peppercorns to a large pot.
2. **Simmer the stock:** Pour water over the ingredients, bring to a boil, then lower the heat to simmer for 3 hours. Skim off foam periodically.
3. **Strain and store:** Strain the stock through a sieve, discard the solids, and let the liquid cool before storing.

Nutritional information per serving: 35 calories, 1 gram fat, 4 grams carbohydrates, 3 grams protein

Expert TIP: Perfect for post-Thanksgiving leftovers. Freeze in small portions for quick soups.

PART II: FROM POT TO BOWL: A COLLECTION OF SOUPS, STEWS AND MORE

MEAT SOUPS

BEEF AND ROOT VEGETABLE STEW

Best season: Winter
Diabetic-friendly, Gluten-free

Servings

6

Preparation Time

15 minutes

Cooking Time

2 hour

YOU WILL NEED:

- 2 tablespoons olive oil (30 milliliters)
- 1 1/2 pounds beef stew meat, cubed (680 grams)
- 1 large onion, diced
- 3 cloves garlic, minced
- 2 large carrots, peeled and chopped
- 2 parsnips, peeled and chopped
- 2 large potatoes, diced
- 6 cups beef stock (1.5 liters)
- 2 tablespoons tomato paste
- 1 teaspoon dried thyme
- 1 teaspoon smoked paprika
- 1 bay leaf
- 1 teaspoon sea salt
- 1/2 teaspoon black pepper

METHOD:

1. **Brown the Beef:** Heat olive oil in a large heavy pot. Add the beef cubes and sear until browned on all sides, about 7-10 minutes. Remove the beef and set aside.
2. **Sauté the Vegetables:** In the same pot, add the onions, garlic, carrots, parsnips, and potatoes. Cook until softened, around 5 minutes.
3. **Simmer the Stew:** Stir in tomato paste, thyme, smoked paprika, bay leaf, salt, and pepper. Pour in the beef stock and return the seared beef to the pot. Bring to a simmer, cover, and cook for 1.5 to 2 hours, until the beef is tender.
4. **Serve:** Adjust seasoning as needed and serve hot.

Nutritional information per serving: 420 calories, 32 grams protein, 15 grams fat, 35 grams carbohydrates

Expert TIP: This stew is perfect for slow cooking. You can also cook it in a slow cooker on low for 8 hours.

BEEF AND KALE SOUP

Best season: Winter
Gluten-free, Diabetic-friendly

Servings

4

Preparation Time

10 minutes

Cooking Time

40 minutes

METHOD:

1. **Brown the Beef:** Heat olive oil in a large pot. Add ground beef and cook until browned, breaking it apart, for about 8 minutes.
2. **Sauté Vegetables:** Stir in onions, garlic, and carrots. Cook for another 5 minutes.
3. **Simmer Soup:** Add beef broth, diced tomatoes, thyme, salt, and pepper. Bring to a boil and simmer for 20 minutes.
4. **Add Kale:** Stir in chopped kale and cook for an additional 5 minutes until wilted.

Nutritional information per serving: 360 calories, 25 grams protein, 18 grams fat, 20 grams carbohydrates

Expert TIP: Kale adds a nutritional boost to this soup while maintaining a nice texture.

YOU WILL NEED:

- 1 tablespoon olive oil (15 milliliters)
- 1 pound ground beef (450 grams)
- 1 medium onion, chopped
- 2 cloves garlic, minced
- 4 cups beef broth (1 liter)
- 2 large carrots, diced
- 1 can diced tomatoes (400 grams)
- 4 cups kale, chopped (240 grams)
- 1 teaspoon dried thyme
- 1/2 teaspoon black pepper
- 1/4 teaspoon sea salt

BEEF AND BLACK BEAN CHILI SOUP

Best season: Fall, Winter
Gluten-Free, Dairy-Free, Diabetic-Friendly

Servings	Preparation Time	Cooking Time
6	15 minutes	40 minutes

YOU WILL NEED:

- 2 tablespoons olive oil (30 milliliters)
- 1 pound lean ground beef (450 grams)
- 1 medium onion, chopped (1 cup, 150 grams)
- 3 cloves garlic, minced
- 1 green bell pepper, diced (1 cup, 150 grams)
- 1 red bell pepper, diced (1 cup, 150 grams)
- 1 can diced tomatoes (15 ounces, 425 grams)
- 1 can black beans, drained and rinsed (15 ounces, 425 grams)
- 4 cups beef broth (950 milliliters)
- 2 tablespoons chili powder
- 1 teaspoon ground cumin
- 1 teaspoon smoked paprika
- 1/2 teaspoon ground black pepper
- 1/2 teaspoon sea salt
- 1/4 teaspoon crushed red pepper flakes (optional)

METHOD:

1. **Brown the beef:** Heat olive oil in a large pot over medium heat. Add ground beef and cook for about 7 minutes, breaking it apart as it browns.
2. **Cook the vegetables:** Stir in the chopped onion, garlic, green and red bell peppers. Sauté for 5 minutes until softened and fragrant.
3. **Add the spices and tomatoes:** Sprinkle in chili powder, cumin, smoked paprika, black pepper, and salt. Stir to coat the beef and vegetables with the spices. Add diced tomatoes and stir well.
4. **Simmer with beans and broth:** Pour in the beef broth and black beans. Bring the soup to a boil, then reduce heat and simmer uncovered for 20 minutes, stirring occasionally to let the flavors meld.
5. **Serve:** Taste and adjust seasoning. Serve hot with a sprinkle of fresh cilantro or a wedge of lime if desired.

Nutritional Information (per serving): 360 calories, 28 grams protein, 20 grams carbohydrates, 18 grams fat, 7 grams fiber

Expert TIP: This chili soup freezes wonderfully. Store in individual portions for quick, hearty meals during the week.

BEEF AND BARLEY SOUP

Best season: Winter
Gluten-free, 30 minutes meal

Servings	Preparation Time	Cooking Time
4	**10 minutes**	**1 hour**

YOU WILL NEED:

- 1 tablespoon olive oil (15 milliliters)
- 1 pound ground beef (450 grams)
- 1 large onion, chopped
- 2 carrots, diced
- 2 celery stalks, diced
- 3 cloves garlic, minced
- 1 cup pearl barley (200 grams)
- 6 cups beef broth (1.5 liters)
- 1 tablespoon fresh thyme leaves
- 1 teaspoon paprika
- 1 teaspoon sea salt
- 1/2 teaspoon black pepper
- 1 bay leaf
- 1/4 cup chopped fresh parsley

METHOD:

1. **Brown the Beef:** In a large pot, heat olive oil over medium heat. Add ground beef and cook until browned, breaking it up as it cooks, about 5 minutes.
2. **Sauté Vegetables:** Stir in the onions, carrots, and celery. Cook for another 7 minutes until vegetables soften.
3. **Add Garlic & Spices:** Add minced garlic, thyme, paprika, salt, pepper, and bay leaf. Stir and cook for an additional minute until fragrant.
4. **Simmer with Broth & Barley:** Pour in the beef broth and stir in the barley. Bring the mixture to a boil, reduce the heat, and simmer for 45 minutes until the barley is tender.
5. **Finish & Serve:** Stir in fresh parsley and adjust seasoning. Serve hot.

Nutritional information per serving: 350 calories, 24 grams protein, 12 grams fat, 40 grams carbohydrates

Expert TIP: This soup freezes well! Make a large batch and freeze individual portions for quick meals later.

BEEF AND RED LENTIL CURRY SOUP

Best season: Fall, Winter
Gluten-Free, Dairy-Free

Servings

6

Preparation Time

15 minutes

Cooking Time

35 minutes

YOU WILL NEED:

- 2 tablespoons olive oil (30 milliliters)
- 1 pound ground beef (450 grams)
- 1 large onion, finely chopped (1 1/2 cups, 225 grams)
- 2 cloves garlic, minced
- 1 tablespoon curry powder (15 grams)
- 1 teaspoon ground turmeric
- 1 teaspoon ground cumin
- 1 teaspoon sea salt
- 1/2 teaspoon ground black pepper
- 1 cup dried red lentils, rinsed (200 grams)
- 6 cups beef broth (1420 milliliters)
- 1 can coconut milk (13.5 ounces, 400 milliliters)
- 1 large tomato, chopped (1 cup, 150 grams)
- 1/4 cup fresh cilantro, chopped (15 grams)

METHOD:

1. **Brown the beef:** Heat olive oil in a large pot over medium heat. Add ground beef and cook for 7-8 minutes, breaking it apart as it browns.
2. **Add spices and vegetables:** Stir in chopped onion and garlic. Cook for 5 minutes, then add curry powder, turmeric, cumin, salt, and black pepper. Cook for another 2 minutes to allow the spices to toast.
3. **Simmer with Lentils:** Stir in the red lentils, beef broth, and chopped tomato. Bring the soup to a boil, then reduce heat and simmer for 25 minutes until the lentils are tender.
4. **Finish with Coconut Milk:** Stir in coconut milk and cook for an additional 5 minutes. Garnish with fresh cilantro before serving.

Nutritional Information (per serving): 460 calories, 25 grams protein, 40 grams carbohydrates, 22 grams fat, 10 grams fiber

Expert TIP: Red lentils cook quickly and add a creamy texture to this rich, spiced soup. If you prefer a thicker soup, mash some of the lentils before serving.

KOREAN-STYLE SPICY BEEF AND KIMCHI SOUP

Best season: Winter
Gluten-Free, Dairy-Free

Servings	Preparation Time	Cooking Time
4	10 minutes	25 minutes

YOU WILL NEED:

- 1 tablespoon sesame oil (15 milliliters)
- 1 pound thinly sliced beef (such as sirloin) (450 grams)
- 2 cloves garlic, minced
- 1 tablespoon gochujang (Korean chili paste) (15 grams)
- 1 tablespoon soy sauce (or tamari for gluten-free) (15 milliliters)
- 1 teaspoon grated ginger (6 grams)
- 4 cups beef broth (950 milliliters)
- 1 cup kimchi, chopped (150 grams)
- 1 block firm tofu, cubed (14 ounces, 400 grams)
- 1 green onion, sliced
- 1 teaspoon toasted sesame seeds

METHOD:

1. **Sear the beef:** Heat sesame oil in a large pot over medium heat. Add the thinly sliced beef and cook for 3-4 minutes until browned.

2. **Add the seasonings:** Stir in minced garlic, gochujang, soy sauce, and grated ginger. Cook for another 2 minutes, letting the spicy and savory aromas fill the kitchen.

3. **Simmer with broth and kimchi:** Pour in the beef broth and add the chopped kimchi. Bring the soup to a boil, then reduce heat and simmer for 15 minutes to allow the flavors to meld.

4. **Finish with tofu and garnishes:** Add cubed tofu and simmer for another 5 minutes to heat through. Serve the soup hot, garnished with sliced green onion and toasted sesame seeds.

Nutritional Information (per serving): 320 calories, 28 grams protein, 12 grams carbohydrates, 18 grams fat, 4 grams fiber

Expert TIP: The fermented kimchi adds probiotics and a unique tangy flavor to the soup. This dish gets better after a day or two in the fridge, as the flavors deepen.

MEDITERRANEAN BEEF AND VEGETABLE SOUP

Best season: Spring, Summer
Dairy-Free, Low Sodium

Servings

4

Preparation Time

15 minutes

Cooking Time

40 minutes

YOU WILL NEED:

- 2 tablespoons olive oil (30 milliliters)
- 1 pound ground beef (450 grams)
- 1 medium zucchini, chopped (1 1/2 cups, 200 grams)
- 1 red bell pepper, chopped (1 cup, 150 grams)
- 1 medium onion, diced (1 cup, 150 grams)
- 3 cloves garlic, minced
- 1/2 teaspoon ground cumin
- 1/2 teaspoon dried oregano
- 1 teaspoon sea salt
- 1/4 teaspoon ground black pepper
- 5 cups low-sodium beef broth (1180 milliliters)
- 1 can diced tomatoes (15 ounces, 425 grams)
- 1/4 cup fresh parsley, chopped (15 grams)

METHOD:

1. **Cook the beef:** Heat olive oil in a large pot over medium heat. Add ground beef and cook for 7-8 minutes, breaking it up as it browns.
2. **Add vegetables and spices:** Stir in zucchini, red bell pepper, onion, and garlic. Cook for 5 minutes until the vegetables soften. Add cumin, oregano, salt, and pepper, and cook for another 2 minutes to allow the spices to bloom.
3. **Simmer the Soup:** Pour in the beef broth and diced tomatoes. Bring to a boil, then reduce heat and let simmer uncovered for 25 minutes, until the vegetables are tender.
4. **Garnish and Serve:** Stir in fresh parsley just before serving for a pop of color and flavor.

Nutritional Information (per serving): 320 calories, 25 grams protein, 18 grams carbohydrates, 18 grams fat, 4 grams fiber

Expert TIP: This low-sodium soup is packed with flavor thanks to the mix of herbs and fresh vegetables. Pair it with a simple salad for a light yet filling meal.

VEAL AND MUSHROOM CHOWDER

Best season: Fall
Gluten-free

Servings

4

Preparation Time

15 minutes

Cooking Time

45 minutes

YOU WILL NEED:

- 2 tablespoons olive oil (30 milliliters)
- 1 pound veal stew meat, cubed (450 grams)
- 1 large onion, diced
- 2 cloves garlic, minced
- 8 ounces mushrooms, sliced (225 grams)
- 2 large potatoes, diced
- 4 cups vegetable broth (1 liter)
- 1 teaspoon dried thyme
- 1 teaspoon sea salt
- 1/2 teaspoon black pepper
- 1 cup heavy cream (240 milliliters)
- 1 tablespoon fresh parsley, chopped

METHOD:

1. **Sear Veal:** Heat olive oil in a large pot over medium heat. Add veal cubes and sear until browned on all sides, about 10 minutes. Remove and set aside.
2. **Cook Vegetables:** In the same pot, sauté onions, garlic, and mushrooms until softened, about 5 minutes.
3. **Simmer Chowder:** Return veal to the pot, add potatoes, vegetable broth, thyme, salt, and pepper. Bring to a boil, reduce heat, and simmer for 30 minutes until veal and potatoes are tender.
4. **Finish with Cream:** Stir in heavy cream and cook for an additional 5 minutes. Garnish with fresh parsley before serving.

Nutritional information per serving: 480 calories, 30 grams protein, 25 grams fat, 35 grams carbohydrates

Expert TIP: The earthy flavor of mushrooms pairs wonderfully with veal. If you like extra texture, stir in some crumbled bacon before serving.

PORK AND FENNEL SOUP

Best season: Fall
Low sodium, Dairy-free

Servings

4

Preparation Time

10 minutes

Cooking Time

45 minutes

YOU WILL NEED:

- 1 tablespoon olive oil (15 milliliters)
- 1 pound pork loin, thinly sliced (450 grams)
- 1 bulb fennel, sliced
- 1 large leek, sliced
- 3 cloves garlic, minced
- 4 cups chicken broth (1 liter)
- 1/2 teaspoon ground fennel seeds
- 1/2 teaspoon black pepper
- 1/4 teaspoon sea salt
- 1 tablespoon fresh parsley, chopped

METHOD:

1. **Sear the Pork:** Heat olive oil in a pot over medium heat. Add pork slices and cook until browned, about 5 minutes.

2. **Cook Fennel and Leek:** Add sliced fennel, leeks, and garlic, and sauté for 5 minutes until softened.

3. **Simmer the Soup:** Add chicken broth, ground fennel, pepper, and salt. Bring to a boil, reduce heat, and simmer for 30 minutes.

4. **Garnish and Serve:** Stir in fresh parsley before serving.

Nutritional information per serving: 320 calories, 28 grams protein, 15 grams fat, 10 grams carbohydrates

Expert TIP: The subtle anise flavor of fennel pairs beautifully with pork, making this soup aromatic and light.

SMOKY CHIPOTLE PORK AND BEAN STEW

Best season: Fall
Gluten-Free, Dairy-Free

Servings

6

Preparation Time

15 minutes

Cooking Time

1 hour

YOU WILL NEED:

- 2 tablespoons olive oil (30 milliliters)
- 1 pound pork shoulder, cubed (450 grams)
- 1 large onion, diced (1 1/2 cups, 225 grams)
- 4 cloves garlic, minced
- 1 chipotle pepper in adobo, chopped (optional for heat)
- 2 cans cannellini beans, drained and rinsed (30 ounces, 850 grams)
- 4 cups chicken broth (950 milliliters)
- 1 can diced tomatoes (15 ounces, 425 grams)
- 1 teaspoon smoked paprika
- 1 teaspoon ground cumin
- 1/2 teaspoon sea salt
- 1/2 teaspoon ground black pepper
- 1/4 cup fresh parsley, chopped (15 grams)

METHOD:

1. **Brown the pork:** Heat olive oil in a large pot over medium-high heat. Add the pork cubes and sear for 6-8 minutes until browned.
2. **Sauté the Vegetables:** Stir in the onion, garlic, and chipotle pepper. Cook for 5 minutes until softened and fragrant.
3. **Add beans and broth:** Stir in the cannellini beans, chicken broth, diced tomatoes, smoked paprika, cumin, salt, and black pepper.
4. **Simmer:** Bring the stew to a boil, then reduce the heat and simmer uncovered for 45 minutes to 1 hour until the pork is tender and the stew has thickened.
5. **Finish with parsley:** Stir in fresh parsley before serving.

Nutritional Information (per serving): 420 calories, 30 grams protein, 30 grams carbohydrates, 18 grams fat, 9 grams fiber

Expert TIP: Chipotle gives this stew a smoky and spicy kick, but you can adjust the heat level by adding more or less. Serve with warm cornbread for a hearty fall dinner.

PORK AND SWEET POTATO STEW

Best season: Winter
Gluten-free, Dairy-free

Servings

6

Preparation Time

15 minutes

Cooking Time

1 hour 20minutes

YOU WILL NEED:

- 2 tablespoons vegetable oil (30 milliliters)
- 1 pound pork shoulder, cubed (450 grams)
- 1 large onion, chopped
- 2 cloves garlic, minced
- 2 medium sweet potatoes, diced
- 2 carrots, diced
- 4 cups chicken broth (1 liter)
- 1 can diced tomatoes (400 grams)
- 1 tablespoon fresh rosemary, chopped
- 1 tablespoon fresh sage, chopped
- 1 teaspoon salt
- 1/2 teaspoon black pepper
- 1/4 teaspoon ground nutmeg

METHOD:

1. **Brown Pork:** In a large pot, heat vegetable oil over medium-high heat. Add cubed pork and sear on all sides until browned, about 7 minutes.
2. **Cook Vegetables:** Add onions and garlic, sauté for 5 minutes until softened.
3. **Simmer Stew:** Stir in sweet potatoes, carrots, chicken broth, and diced tomatoes. Add rosemary, sage, salt, pepper, and nutmeg. Bring to a boil, then reduce heat and **simmer uncovered for 1 hour until pork is tender.**
4. **Serve:** Adjust seasoning if necessary and serve the stew hot.

Nutritional information per serving: 390 calories, 26 grams protein, 14 grams fat, 35 grams carbohydrates

Expert TIP: Sweet potatoes give a natural sweetness to the stew, balancing the savory pork perfectly. Freeze leftovers for quick meals.

CREAMY PORK AND POTATO CHOWDER

Best season: Winter
Gluten-Free

Servings

6

Preparation
Time

15 minutes

Cooking
Time

40 minutes

YOU WILL NEED:

- 2 tablespoons butter (30 grams)
- 1 pound ground pork (450 grams)
- 1 large onion, diced (1 ½ cups, 225 grams)
- 2 medium potatoes, peeled and cubed (3 cups, 600 grams)
- 2 cloves garlic, minced
- 4 cups chicken broth (950 milliliters)
- 1 1/2 cups heavy cream (360 milliliters)
- 1 teaspoon dried thyme
- 1/2 teaspoon ground black pepper
- 1 teaspoon sea salt
- 1/4 cup fresh parsley, chopped (15 grams)
- 1/4 teaspoon cayenne pepper (optional for heat)

METHOD:

1. **Brown the pork:** Melt the butter in a large pot over medium heat. Add ground pork and cook for 7-8 minutes, breaking it up as it browns.

2. **Sauté Vegetables:** Stir in the diced onion, garlic, and potatoes. Cook for 5 minutes, stirring occasionally until the vegetables soften slightly.

3. **Simmer the Chowder:** Pour in the chicken broth and add the thyme, salt, and pepper. Bring the chowder to a boil, then reduce the heat and simmer for 25 minutes until the potatoes are tender.

4. **Finish with Cream:** Stir in the heavy cream and cayenne pepper, if using, and cook for an additional 5 minutes. Taste and adjust seasoning as needed.

5. **Garnish and Serve:** Stir in fresh parsley before serving. Enjoy with crusty gluten-free bread.

Nutritional Information (per serving): 500 calories, 28 grams protein, 35 grams carbohydrates, 28 grams fat, 4 grams fiber

Expert TIP: This chowder has a rich, creamy texture. If you prefer a lighter option, swap heavy cream for coconut milk for a dairy-free variation.

LEMON-GINGER PORK AND VEGETABLE STIR-FRY SOUP

Best season: Spring
Gluten-Free, Dairy-Free, Low Sodium

Servings
4

Preparation Time
10 minutes

Cooking Time
25 minutes

YOU WILL NEED:

- 1 tablespoon sesame oil (15 milliliters)
- 1 pound pork loin, thinly sliced (450 grams)
- 1 tablespoon fresh ginger, grated (6 grams)
- 2 cloves garlic, minced
- 1 medium zucchini, sliced (1 1/2 cups, 200 grams)
- 1 medium red bell pepper, julienned (1 cup, 150 grams)
- 1 cup snow peas, trimmed (100 grams)
- 4 cups chicken broth (950 milliliters)
- 2 tablespoons low-sodium soy sauce (30 milliliters, or tamari for gluten-free)
- 1 tablespoon lemon juice (15 milliliters)
- 1 teaspoon sesame seeds
- 1/4 cup fresh basil, chopped (15 grams)

METHOD:

1. **Sear the pork:** Heat sesame oil in a large pot over medium heat. Add the sliced pork and cook for 5 minutes until browned.

2. **Add aromatics and vegetables:** Stir in the grated ginger, minced garlic, zucchini, red bell pepper, and snow peas. Cook for 5 minutes until vegetables start to soften.

3. **Simmer the Broth:** Pour in the chicken broth and soy sauce. Bring to a boil, then lower the heat and simmer for 10 minutes.

4. **Finish with lemon and basil:** Stir in lemon juice and fresh basil just before serving. Garnish with sesame seeds.

Nutritional Information (per serving): 320 calories, 28 grams protein, 15 grams carbohydrates, 15 grams fat, 4 grams fiber

Expert TIP: This light and refreshing soup is perfect for spring. Serve with a side of jasmine rice or rice noodles for a heartier meal.

PORK AND APPLE CIDER STEW

Best season: Fall
Gluten-free, Diabetic-friendly

Servings
6

Preparation Time
15 minutes

Cooking Time
1 hour 30 minutes

YOU WILL NEED:

- 2 tablespoons olive oil (30 milliliters)
- 1 1/2 pounds pork shoulder, cubed (680 grams)
- 1 large onion, diced
- 3 cloves garlic, minced
- 2 large apples, peeled and sliced
- 2 medium carrots, sliced
- 4 cups chicken broth (1 liter)
- 1 cup apple cider (240 milliliters)
- 1 teaspoon dried sage
- 1 teaspoon sea salt
- 1/2 teaspoon black pepper
- 1 tablespoon fresh thyme, chopped

METHOD:

1. **Brown the Pork:** Heat olive oil in a large pot over medium-high heat. Add pork cubes and brown on all sides, about 8 minutes.

2. **Sauté Vegetables:** Add onions, garlic, apples, and carrots to the pot and cook for 5 minutes until softened.

3. **Simmer with Broth and Cider:** Pour in chicken broth and apple cider. Add sage, salt, pepper, and thyme. Bring to a boil, then reduce heat and simmer for 1.5 hours until the pork is tender.

4. **Serve:** Adjust seasoning if needed and serve hot.

Nutritional information per serving: 400 calories, 28 grams protein, 18 grams fat, 30 grams carbohydrates

Expert TIP: The apple cider adds a sweet contrast to the savory pork, making this stew a true autumn comfort food.

PORK, APPLE, AND CABBAGE STEW

Best season: Winter
Gluten-Free, Dairy-Free

Servings
6

Preparation Time
15 minutes

Cooking Time
1 hour 15 minutes

YOU WILL NEED:

- 2 tablespoons olive oil (30 milliliters)
- 1 ½ pounds pork shoulder, cut into 1-inch cubes (680 grams)
- 1 large onion, diced (1 ½ cups, 225 grams)
- 2 Granny Smith apples, peeled and chopped (2 cups, 300 grams)
- 1 small head of green cabbage, chopped (4 cups, 600 grams)
- 4 cloves garlic, minced
- 1 tablespoon Dijon mustard (15 grams)
- 1 tablespoon apple cider vinegar (15 milliliters)
- 6 cups chicken broth (1420 milliliters)
- 1 bay leaf
- 1 teaspoon sea salt
- 1/2 teaspoon ground black pepper
- 1 teaspoon dried thyme

METHOD:

1. **Brown the pork:** Heat olive oil in a large pot over medium-high heat. Add the pork cubes and brown on all sides for 8 minutes.

2. **Sauté the onions and apples:** Stir in the diced onion and chopped apples. Cook for 5 minutes until softened.

3. **Add cabbage and seasonings:** Stir in the chopped cabbage, garlic, Dijon mustard, apple cider vinegar, bay leaf, thyme, salt, and black pepper. Cook for another 3 minutes.

4. **Simmer the Stew:** Pour in the chicken broth, bring to a boil, then reduce heat and simmer covered for 1 hour until the pork is tender and the flavors meld.

5. **Serve:** Discard the bay leaf before serving. Adjust seasoning and enjoy.

Nutritional Information (per serving): 380 calories, 28 grams protein, 20 grams carbohydrates, 18 grams fat, 6 grams fiber

Expert TIP: The apple adds a subtle sweetness that balances the savory pork and cabbage. This dish pairs well with roasted potatoes or crusty gluten-free bread.

SPICY PORK AND HOMINY STEW (POZOLE ROJO)

Best season: Fall, Winter
Gluten-Free, Dairy-Free

Servings	Preparation Time	Cooking Time

8	20 minutes	1 hour 30 minutes

YOU WILL NEED:

- 2 tablespoons vegetable oil (30 milliliters)
- 2 pounds pork shoulder, cut into chunks (900 grams)
- 1 large onion, chopped (1 1/2 cups, 225 grams)
- 4 cloves garlic, minced
- 3 dried ancho chilies, stemmed and seeded
- 2 dried guajillo chilies, stemmed and seeded
- 8 cups chicken broth (1.9 liters)
- 2 cans hominy, drained and rinsed (30 ounces, 850 grams)
- 1 tablespoon oregano
- 1 teaspoon sea salt
- 1/2 teaspoon ground black pepper
- 2 tablespoons lime juice (30 milliliters)

METHOD:

1. **Brown the pork:** Heat vegetable oil in a large pot over medium heat. Add pork chunks and brown on all sides for 8-10 minutes.

2. **Toast and blend the chilies:** Meanwhile, in a dry skillet, toast the ancho and guajillo chilies for 2 minutes until fragrant. Transfer to a bowl, cover with hot water, and let them soften for 10 minutes. Blend the chilies with a little soaking water until smooth.

3. **Add aromatics and broth:** Stir in the chopped onion and garlic with the pork, cooking for 5 minutes. Add the chili paste, chicken broth, hominy, oregano, salt, and black pepper.

4. **Simmer:** Bring to a boil, then reduce heat and simmer uncovered for 1 1/2 hours until the pork is tender and the flavors are well combined.

5. **Finish and Serve:** Stir in lime juice just before serving. Garnish with chopped radishes, shredded cabbage, and cilantro for an authentic experience.

Nutritional Information (per serving): 390 calories, 25 grams protein, 35 grams carbohydrates, 16 grams fat, 8 grams fiber

Expert TIP: Pozole is traditionally served with a variety of garnishes like avocado, sliced radishes, and shredded lettuce. You can make this a day ahead—the flavors intensify overnight.

SOUTHWEST BEEF AND CORN CHOWDER

Best season: Fall
Gluten-free, 30 minutes meal

Servings	Preparation Time	Cooking Time
4	15 minutes	25 minutes

YOU WILL NEED:

- 1 tablespoon olive oil (15 milliliters)
- 1 pound ground beef (450 grams)
- 1 small onion, diced
- 2 cloves garlic, minced
- 2 large russet potatoes, diced
- 1 cup frozen corn (150 grams)
- 1 red bell pepper, chopped
- 4 cups beef broth (1 liter)
- 1 can diced tomatoes with green chiles (400 grams)
- 1 teaspoon ground cumin
- 1 teaspoon smoked paprika
- 1/2 teaspoon chili powder
- 1 teaspoon sea salt
- 1/2 teaspoon black pepper
- 1/2 cup heavy cream (120 milliliters)
- 2 tablespoons fresh cilantro, chopped (optional)

METHOD:

1. **Brown the Beef:** In a large pot, heat olive oil over medium heat. Add ground beef and cook until browned, breaking it up with a spoon, about 7-8 minutes. Drain any excess fat.

2. **Sauté Vegetables:** Add diced onions and garlic to the pot, cooking until softened, about 3 minutes. Stir in the red bell pepper and potatoes, cooking for another 5 minutes.

3. **Simmer with Spices:** Stir in cumin, smoked paprika, chili powder, salt, and pepper. Pour in the beef broth and canned tomatoes with green chiles. Bring to a boil, then reduce heat and simmer for 15 minutes, or until the potatoes are tender.

4. **Add Corn and Cream:** Stir in the corn and heavy cream, cooking for an additional 5 minutes until the chowder thickens slightly.

5. **Serve:** Ladle the chowder into bowls and garnish with fresh cilantro, if desired. Serve with warm cornbread for a full meal.

Nutritional information per serving: 480 calories, 28 grams protein, 26 grams fat, 35 grams carbohydrates

Expert TIP: Adding the canned tomatoes with green chiles brings a Southwestern kick to this chowder. For extra heat, top with sliced jalapeños.

VEAL AND SPINACH SOUP

Best season: Spring
Low sodium, Diabetic-friendly

Servings	Preparation Time	Cooking Time
4	10 minutes	30 minutes

YOU WILL NEED:

- 1 tablespoon olive oil (15 milliliters)
- 1 pound ground veal (450 grams)
- 1 small onion, finely diced
- 2 cloves garlic, minced
- 1 large carrot, grated
- 4 cups vegetable broth (1 liter)
- 1 can diced tomatoes (400 grams)
- 1/2 teaspoon dried oregano
- 1/4 teaspoon black pepper
- 4 cups fresh spinach (240 grams)
- 1 tablespoon lemon juice

METHOD:

1. **Cook the Veal:** In a large pot, heat olive oil over medium heat. Add the ground veal and cook, breaking it apart, until browned, about 8 minutes.

2. **Sauté Vegetables:** Stir in onions, garlic, and grated carrot. Cook until softened, about 5 minutes.

3. **Simmer the Soup:** Add vegetable broth, diced tomatoes, oregano, and black pepper. Bring to a boil, then reduce heat and simmer for 15 minutes.

4. **Add Spinach and Lemon:** Stir in the spinach and cook until wilted, about 2 minutes. Finish with lemon juice and serve.

Nutritional information per serving: 280 calories, 26 grams protein, 12 grams fat, 20 grams carbohydrates

Expert TIP: This light soup is great for spring but can be enjoyed year-round. You can also use kale instead of spinach for extra nutrients.

LAMB CHOWDER

Best season: Fall / Winter

Servings	Preparation Time	Cooking Time
4	**15 minutes**	**30 minutes**

YOU WILL NEED:

- 2 tablespoons olive oil (30 milliliters)
- 1 pound lamb shoulder, cubed (450 grams)
- 1 large yellow onion, chopped (about 1 1/2 cups or 200 grams)
- 2 cloves garlic, minced
- 3 large carrots, peeled and diced (about 1 1/2 cups or 225 grams)
- 2 large celery stalks, diced (about 1 cup or 100 grams)
- 2 medium potatoes, peeled and cubed (about 2 cups or 300 grams)
- 1 teaspoon dried thyme
- 1 teaspoon smoked paprika
- 1/2 teaspoon ground black pepper
- 1/2 teaspoon sea salt
- 4 cups lamb or vegetable broth (950 milliliters)
- 1 bay leaf
- 1/2 cup coconut milk (120 milliliters)
- Fresh parsley, chopped, for garnish

METHOD:

1. **Sear the Lamb:** In a large pot, heat olive oil over medium-high heat. Add cubed lamb and sear on all sides until browned, about 5-6 minutes. This will help develop deep flavors.

2. **Sauté Vegetables:** Add chopped onion and minced garlic to the pot with the lamb. Cook for 3 minutes until onions are translucent and garlic is fragrant.

3. **Add Carrots, Celery, and Potatoes:** Stir in diced carrots, celery, and potatoes. Let the vegetables cook for about 4-5 minutes, softening them slightly.

4. **Season and Simmer:** Add thyme, smoked paprika, black pepper, and sea salt. Pour in the broth and add the bay leaf. Bring the mixture to a boil, then reduce to a simmer. Cover and cook for 20 minutes, allowing the vegetables to become tender and the lamb to fully cook through.

5. **Finish with Coconut Milk:** Once the lamb is tender and the vegetables are cooked, stir in the coconut milk to give the chowder a creamy texture. Simmer for an additional 5 minutes, letting the flavors meld.

6. **Serve:** Ladle the lamb chowder into bowls and garnish with fresh parsley for a bright, fresh finish.

Nutritional information per serving: 340 calories, 18 grams fat, 30 grams carbohydrates, 22 grams protein, 550 milligrams sodium

Expert TIP: This chowder freezes well. Store leftovers in an airtight container for up to 3 months. For a thicker chowder, mash a few of the potatoes before serving.

MOROCCAN LAMB AND CHICKPEA SOUP

Best season: Fall
Gluten-free, Dairy-free

Servings

Preparation Time

Cooking Time

4   **15 minutes**   **1 hour**

YOU WILL NEED:

- 2 tablespoons olive oil (30 milliliters)
- 1 pound ground lamb (450 grams)
- 1 large onion, diced
- 3 cloves garlic, minced
- 1 teaspoon ground cumin
- 1 teaspoon ground coriander
- 1/2 teaspoon ground cinnamon
- 1/2 teaspoon ground turmeric
- 1/4 teaspoon cayenne pepper (optional)
- 1 can chickpeas, drained and rinsed (400 grams)
- 1 can diced tomatoes (400 grams)
- 4 cups chicken or vegetable broth (1 liter)
- 1/2 teaspoon salt
- 1/4 teaspoon black pepper
- 1/4 cup fresh cilantro, chopped
- 1 lemon, cut into wedges

METHOD:

1. **Cook the Lamb:** Heat the olive oil in a large pot over medium heat. Add the lamb and cook until browned, breaking it up as it cooks, around 8 minutes.

2. **Add the Spices:** Stir in onions and garlic and cook until softened, about 5 minutes. Add cumin, coriander, cinnamon, turmeric, and cayenne (if using), and cook until fragrant, about 1 minute.

3. **Simmer:** Add the chickpeas, diced tomatoes, broth, salt, and pepper. Bring to a boil, then reduce heat and simmer for 45 minutes to let the flavors meld.

4. **Finish and Serve:** Stir in fresh cilantro and serve with lemon wedges.

Nutritional information per serving: 380 calories, 25 grams protein, 15 grams fat, 35 grams carbohydrates

Expert TIP: Adding a squeeze of lemon right before eating brightens the rich flavors of this soup.

SPICY LAMB AND TOMATO SOUP

Best season: Fall
Gluten-free, Dairy-free

Servings

4

Preparation
Time

10 minutes

Cooking
Time

40 minutes

YOU WILL NEED:

- 1 tablespoon olive oil (15 milliliters)
- 1 pound ground lamb (450 grams)
- 1 large onion, diced
- 3 cloves garlic, minced
- 2 teaspoons ground cumin
- 1/2 teaspoon ground cinnamon
- 1/4 teaspoon cayenne pepper (optional)
- 4 cups vegetable broth (1 liter)
- 2 cans diced tomatoes (800 grams)
- 1/2 teaspoon sea salt
- 1/4 teaspoon black pepper
- 2 tablespoons fresh mint, chopped

METHOD:

1. **Brown the Lamb:** In a large pot, heat olive oil over medium heat. Add ground lamb and cook until browned, about 8 minutes.

2. **Add Spices:** Stir in onions, garlic, cumin, cinnamon, and cayenne. Cook until fragrant, about 5 minutes.

3. **Simmer with Tomatoes:** Add vegetable broth, diced tomatoes, salt, and pepper. Bring to a boil, reduce heat, and simmer for 30 minutes.

4. **Finish and Serve:** Stir in fresh mint before serving.

Nutritional information per serving: 410 calories, 28 grams protein, 20 grams fat, 25 grams carbohydrates

Expert TIP: For a heartier meal, serve this soup with warm flatbread to soak up the rich flavors.

CUBAN-STYLE PORK AND BLACK BEAN SOUP

Best season: Winter
Gluten-Free, Dairy-Free

Servings

6

Preparation
Time

15 minutes

Cooking
Time

45 minutes

YOU WILL NEED:

- 2 tablespoons olive oil (30 milliliters)
- 1 pound pork tenderloin, cut into cubes (450 grams)
- 1 large onion, diced (1 1/2 cups, 225 grams)
- 1 green bell pepper, chopped (1 cup, 150 grams)
- 4 cloves garlic, minced
- 2 teaspoons ground cumin
- 1 teaspoon smoked paprika
- 1 teaspoon dried oregano
- 1/2 teaspoon ground black pepper
- 1 teaspoon sea salt
- 4 cups chicken broth (950 milliliters)
- 2 cans black beans, drained and rinsed (30 ounces, 850 grams)
- 1/4 cup lime juice (60 milliliters)
- 1/4 cup fresh cilantro, chopped (15 grams)

METHOD:

1. **Sear the pork:** Heat olive oil in a large pot over medium-high heat. Add the pork cubes and brown for 5-7 minutes until golden.

2. **Sauté the Vegetables:** Add the diced onion, green bell pepper, and garlic. Cook for 5 minutes until softened and fragrant.

3. **Add spices and broth:** Stir in cumin, smoked paprika, oregano, black pepper, and salt. Pour in the chicken broth, then bring to a boil.

4. **Simmer with beans:** Add the black beans, reduce heat, and simmer for 30 minutes to allow flavors to meld and the pork to become tender.

5. **Finish with lime and cilantro:** Stir in the lime juice and cilantro before serving.

Nutritional Information (per serving): 360 calories, 30 grams protein, 25 grams carbohydrates, 12 grams fat, 10 grams fiber

Expert TIP: For a Cuban twist, serve with rice and a dollop of sour cream or avocado slices. This soup freezes well for up to 3 months.

Best season: Winter
30 minutes meal, Gluten-free

Servings	Preparation Time	Cooking Time
4	10 minutes	20 minutes

YOU WILL NEED:

- 1 tablespoon olive oil (15 milliliters)
- 1 small onion, diced
- 2 cloves garlic, minced
- 2 cups cooked ham, diced (300 grams)
- 2 cans white beans, drained and rinsed (800 grams)
- 3 medium potatoes, diced
- 4 cups chicken broth (1 liter)
- 1/2 teaspoon dried thyme
- 1/2 teaspoon smoked paprika
- 1/4 teaspoon black pepper
- 1/2 cup heavy cream (120 milliliters)
- 2 tablespoons fresh parsley, chopped

METHOD:

1. **Sauté the Vegetables:** Heat olive oil in a large pot over medium heat. Add onions and garlic, and cook until softened, about 5 minutes.

2. **Add Ham and Potatoes:** Stir in the ham, potatoes, white beans, thyme, paprika, and black pepper. Cook for 5 minutes.

3. **Simmer the Chowder:** Pour in chicken broth and bring to a boil. Reduce heat and simmer for 10-15 minutes until the potatoes are tender.

4. **Add Cream and Serve:** Stir in the heavy cream and heat through, then sprinkle with parsley before serving.

Nutritional information per serving: 450 calories, 28 grams protein, 18 grams fat, 45 grams carbohydrates

Expert TIP: This hearty chowder is a great way to use up leftover holiday ham.

SMOKEY HAM AND CORN CHOWDER

Best season: Fall
Gluten-free, 30 minutes meal

Servings

4

Preparation Time

10 minutes

Cooking Time

20 minutes

YOU WILL NEED:

- 2 tablespoons unsalted butter (30 grams)
- 1 medium onion, diced
- 2 cloves garlic, minced
- 2 cups diced cooked ham (300 grams)
- 2 large potatoes, diced
- 4 cups chicken broth (1 liter)
- 3 cups corn kernels, fresh or frozen (450 grams)
- 1 teaspoon smoked paprika
- 1 teaspoon salt
- 1/2 teaspoon black pepper
- 1 cup heavy cream (240 milliliters)
- 2 green onions, thinly sliced for garnish

METHOD:

1. **Sauté Onion & Garlic:** Melt butter in a large pot over medium heat. Add onions and garlic, cooking until soft, about 5 minutes.
2. **Add Ham & Potatoes:** Stir in diced ham and potatoes. Cook for another 5 minutes, allowing the flavors to meld.
3. **Add Broth & Corn:** Pour in the chicken broth and stir in corn. Bring to a boil, then lower heat and simmer for 10 minutes until the potatoes are tender.
4. **Finish with Cream:** Stir in the smoked paprika, salt, pepper, and heavy cream. Simmer for 5 minutes before serving. Garnish with green onions.

Nutritional information per serving: 450 calories, 25 grams protein, 20 grams fat, 50 grams carbohydrates

Expert TIP: For a lighter version, replace heavy cream with milk. This chowder tastes even better the next day after flavors meld.

SAVORY GOAT AND WHITE BEAN STEW

Best season: Spring, Winter
Gluten-Free, Dairy-Free, Low Sodium

Servings

4

Preparation Time

15 minutes

Cooking Time

6 hours

YOU WILL NEED:

- 2 tablespoons olive oil (30 milliliters)
- 1 1/2 pounds goat meat, cubed (680 grams)
- 1 large onion, chopped (1 1/2 cups, 225 grams)
- 4 cloves garlic, minced
- 2 medium carrots, chopped (1 cup, 125 grams)
- 1 can white beans, drained and rinsed (15 ounces, 425 grams)
- 6 cups chicken or goat broth (1420 milliliters)
- 1 teaspoon ground cumin
- 1 teaspoon ground coriander
- 1/2 teaspoon ground turmeric
- 1 bay leaf
- 1 teaspoon sea salt
- 1/2 teaspoon ground black pepper
- 1/4 cup fresh cilantro, chopped (15 grams)

METHOD:

1. **Brown the goat:** Heat olive oil in a large pot over medium-high heat. Add the goat meat and brown for 8-10 minutes until well-seared.
2. **Cook vegetables and spices:** Stir in the onion, garlic, and carrots. Cook for 5 minutes, then add cumin, coriander, turmeric, salt, and black pepper. Cook for 2 more minutes to release the spices' flavors.
3. **Simmer with beans:** Add the white beans, broth, and bay leaf. Bring to a boil, then lower the heat, cover, and simmer for 1 1/2 to 2 hours until the goat is tender.
4. **Finish and Serve:** Stir in fresh cilantro just before serving. Adjust seasoning to taste and serve the stew warm.

Nutritional Information (per serving): 460 calories, 38 grams protein, 25 grams carbohydrates, 20 grams fat, 8 grams fiber

Expert TIP: Goat is a lean meat that absorbs the rich flavors of spices and beans well. For a heartier stew, add cubed potatoes or a handful of spinach near the end of cooking.

POULTRY SOUPS

DUCK AND MUSHROOM SOUP

Best season: Winter
Gluten-free, Dairy-free

Servings	Preparation Time	Cooking Time

4	10 minutes	45 minutes

YOU WILL NEED:

- 1 tablespoon duck fat or olive oil (15 milliliters)
- 1 pound duck breast, skin removed, cubed (450 grams)
- 1 small onion, chopped
- 2 cloves garlic, minced
- 8 ounces cremini mushrooms, sliced (225 grams)
- 3 medium carrots, diced
- 4 cups chicken broth (1 liter)
- 1/2 teaspoon dried thyme
- 1/2 teaspoon sea salt
- 1/4 teaspoon black pepper
- 1/4 cup fresh parsley, chopped

METHOD:

1. **Sear the Duck:** In a large pot, heat duck fat or olive oil over medium-high heat. Add the cubed duck breast and sear until browned, about 7 minutes. Remove and set aside.

2. **Sauté Vegetables:** In the same pot, sauté onions, garlic, mushrooms, and carrots for 5 minutes until softened.

3. **Simmer Soup:** Stir in chicken broth, thyme, salt, and pepper. Bring to a boil, reduce heat, and simmer for 35 minutes.

4. **Finish and Serve:** Stir in the seared duck and fresh parsley before serving.

Nutritional information per serving: 480 calories, 35 grams protein, 20 grams fat, 20 grams carbohydrates

Expert TIP: Duck adds a rich, savory flavor to this hearty winter soup. For extra depth, stir in a splash of sherry vinegar before serving.

CRISPY DUCK AND ORANGE BARLEY STEW

Best season: Winter
Gluten-free

Servings	Preparation Time	Cooking Time

4	15 minutes	1 hour 30 minutes

YOU WILL NEED:

- 2 duck legs, bone-in, skin on (about 1 pound or 450 grams)
- 1 tablespoon olive oil (15 milliliters)
- 1 small onion, diced
- 2 cloves garlic, minced
- 1 cup pearl barley (200 grams)
- 4 cups chicken broth (1 liter)
- 1 large carrot, diced
- 1 celery stalk, diced
- 1 orange, zest and juice
- 1 teaspoon dried thyme
- 1/2 teaspoon sea salt
- 1/4 teaspoon black pepper
- 1/4 cup fresh parsley, chopped

METHOD:

1. **Crisp the Duck:** Heat olive oil in a large, deep pot over medium heat. Place the duck legs skin side down and cook until the skin is golden and crispy, about 8 minutes. Flip the duck and cook for another 5 minutes. Remove and set aside.

2. **Sauté Vegetables:** In the same pot, add diced onion, garlic, carrot, and celery. Cook for 5 minutes until softened.

3. **Simmer with Barley:** Add pearl barley, chicken broth, thyme, salt, and pepper. Stir in orange zest and juice. Return the duck legs to the pot, cover, and simmer for 1 hour until the barley is tender and the duck is fully cooked.

4. **Shred Duck:** Remove duck legs from the pot, shred the meat, and discard the bones. Return the shredded duck to the stew.

5. **Finish and Serve:** Stir in fresh parsley and adjust seasoning. Serve warm with extra orange zest on top for a bright finish.

Nutritional information per serving: 540 calories, 30 grams protein, 24 grams fat, 45 grams carbohydrates

Expert TIP: The orange adds a fresh citrusy flavor that cuts through the richness of the duck, while the barley gives the stew a hearty, comforting texture.

CREAMY CHICKEN AND WILD RICE SOUP

Best season: Winter
Gluten-free

Servings	Preparation Time	Cooking Time

6	15 minutes	45 minutes

YOU WILL NEED:

- 2 tablespoons unsalted butter (30 grams)
- 1 pound boneless, skinless chicken thighs, cubed (450 grams)
- 1 large carrot, diced
- 2 celery stalks, diced
- 1 onion, chopped
- 1 cup wild rice (200 grams)
- 6 cups chicken broth (1.5 liters)
- 1 teaspoon dried thyme
- 1 teaspoon sea salt
- 1/2 teaspoon black pepper
- 1 cup heavy cream (240 milliliters)
- 2 tablespoons fresh parsley, chopped

METHOD:

1. **Brown the Chicken:** In a large pot, melt the butter over medium heat. Add the cubed chicken thighs and cook until browned, about 8 minutes. Remove and set aside.

2. **Cook Vegetables:** Sauté the diced carrots, celery, and onion in the same pot for 5 minutes until softened.

3. **Simmer with Rice:** Add the wild rice, chicken broth, thyme, salt, and pepper. Bring to a boil, then reduce heat and simmer for 35 minutes until the rice is tender.

4. **Add Cream and Chicken:** Stir in the cooked chicken and heavy cream. Simmer for an additional 5 minutes. Garnish with parsley before serving.

Nutritional information per serving: 450 calories, 26 grams protein, 20 grams fat, 40 grams carbohydrates

Expert TIP: This soup thickens as it cools, so add a splash of broth or water when reheating for leftovers.

SMOKY CHICKEN AND BLACK BEAN CHOWDER

Best season: Fall
Dairy-free

Servings

4

Preparation Time

15 minutes

Cooking Time

25 minutes

YOU WILL NEED:

- 1 tablespoon olive oil (15 milliliters)
- 1 pound boneless, skinless chicken breasts, cubed (450 grams)
- 1 small onion, diced
- 1 red bell pepper, diced
- 2 cloves garlic, minced
- 1 can black beans, drained and rinsed (400 grams)
- 1 can diced tomatoes (400 grams)
- 4 cups chicken broth (1 liter)
- 1 teaspoon ground cumin
- 1 teaspoon smoked paprika
- 1/2 teaspoon sea salt
- 1/4 teaspoon black pepper
- 1/4 cup fresh cilantro, chopped

METHOD:

1. **Brown the Chicken:** In a large pot, heat olive oil over medium heat. Add cubed chicken and cook until browned, about 7 minutes. Remove and set aside.

2. **Sauté Vegetables:** Stir in onions, red bell pepper, and garlic, cooking for 5 minutes until softened.

3. **Simmer the Chowder:** Add black beans, diced tomatoes, chicken broth, cumin, paprika, salt, and pepper. Bring to a boil, reduce heat, and simmer for 15 minutes.

4. **Finish and Serve:** Stir in the cooked chicken and cilantro just before serving.

Nutritional information per serving: 320 calories, 28 grams protein, 8 grams fat, 35 grams carbohydrates

Expert TIP: This chowder is packed with smoky flavor thanks to the paprika. Top with avocado slices for added creaminess.

CHICKEN AND SWEET POTATO CHOWDER

Best season: Winter
Gluten-free, 30 minutes meal

Servings

4

Preparation Time

10 minutes

Cooking Time

20 hours

YOU WILL NEED:

- 1 tablespoon olive oil (15 milliliters)
- 1 pound boneless, skinless chicken thighs, cubed (450 grams)
- 1 large sweet potato, peeled and diced
- 1 medium onion, chopped
- 2 cloves garlic, minced
- 4 cups chicken broth (1 liter)
- 1/2 teaspoon ground cumin
- 1/2 teaspoon smoked paprika
- 1/2 teaspoon sea salt
- 1/4 teaspoon black pepper
- 1 cup coconut milk (240 milliliters)
- 2 tablespoons fresh parsley, chopped

METHOD:

1. **Brown the Chicken:** Heat olive oil in a large pot over medium heat. Add chicken and cook for 6-8 minutes, until browned. Remove and set aside.

2. **Cook Vegetables:** In the same pot, sauté the diced sweet potato, onion, and garlic for 5 minutes until softened.

3. **Simmer the Chowder:** Stir in the chicken broth, cumin, paprika, salt, and pepper. Bring to a boil, then reduce heat and simmer for 10 minutes, or until the sweet potatoes are tender.

4. **Add Coconut Milk:** Stir in the coconut milk and cooked chicken, and simmer for an additional 5 minutes. Garnish with fresh parsley before serving.

Nutritional information per serving: 420 calories, 30 grams protein, 15 grams fat, 35 grams carbohydrates

Expert TIP: The coconut milk adds creaminess without dairy, making this chowder rich and perfect for those chilly winter nights.

CHICKEN, FENNEL, AND APPLE STEW

Best season: Fall
Gluten-free, Dairy-free

Servings

4

Preparation Time

10 minutes

Cooking Time

1 hour

YOU WILL NEED:

- 2 tablespoons olive oil (30 milliliters)
- 1 pound boneless, skinless chicken thighs, cubed (450 grams)
- 1 large fennel bulb, thinly sliced
- 1 large apple, peeled and diced
- 1 small onion, diced
- 2 cloves garlic, minced
- 4 cups chicken broth (1 liter)
- 1 teaspoon dried thyme
- 1/2 teaspoon sea salt
- 1/4 teaspoon black pepper
- 1 tablespoon apple cider vinegar
- 2 tablespoons fresh parsley, chopped

METHOD:

1. **Brown the Chicken:** Heat olive oil in a large pot over medium-high heat. Add chicken and cook until browned, about 7 minutes. Remove and set aside.

2. **Cook Vegetables:** In the same pot, sauté fennel, apple, onion, and garlic for 5 minutes until softened.

3. **Simmer the Stew:** Stir in chicken broth, thyme, salt, and pepper. Return the chicken to the pot and bring to a boil. Reduce heat, cover, and simmer for 45 minutes.

4. **Finish and Serve:** Stir in apple cider vinegar and garnish with fresh parsley before serving.

Nutritional information per serving: 380 calories, 28 grams protein, 15 grams fat, 35 grams carbohydrates

Expert TIP: The sweetness from the apple balances the savory fennel and chicken, making this stew perfect for cozy fall dinners.

Best season: Winter
Gluten-free, Dairy-free

Servings

Preparation Time

Cooking Time

4   **15 minutes**   **25 minutes**

YOU WILL NEED:

- 1 tablespoon coconut oil (15 milliliters)
- 1 pound boneless, skinless chicken thighs, cubed (450 grams)
- 1 small onion, diced
- 2 cloves garlic, minced
- 1 tablespoon fresh ginger, grated
- 1 tablespoon red curry paste
- 1 can coconut milk (400 milliliters)
- 4 cups chicken broth (1 liter)
- 1 red bell pepper, thinly sliced
- 1 small sweet potato, diced
- 1 tablespoon fish sauce (optional)
- 1 teaspoon sea salt
- 1/2 teaspoon black pepper
- 2 tablespoons fresh cilantro, chopped
- 1 lime, cut into wedges

METHOD:

1. **Sear the Chicken:** Heat coconut oil in a large pot over medium heat. Add chicken and cook for 5-7 minutes, until browned. Remove and set aside.

2. **Sauté Aromatics:** Add onion, garlic, and ginger to the pot. Cook for 3 minutes, then stir in red curry paste.

3. **Simmer the Soup:** Pour in coconut milk, chicken broth, red bell pepper, sweet potato, fish sauce (if using), salt, and pepper. Bring to a boil, reduce heat, and simmer for 15 minutes until vegetables are tender.

4. **Add Chicken and Serve:** Return the chicken to the pot and heat through. Serve with fresh cilantro and lime wedges.

Nutritional information per serving: 420 calories, 30 grams protein, 22 grams fat, 25 grams carbohydrates

Expert TIP: The sweetness of the coconut milk and sweet potato balances the heat of the curry paste. This soup is both warming and creamy.

CHICKEN AND ARTICHOKE CHOWDER

Best season: Spring
Gluten-free

Servings

4

Preparation
Time

10 minutes

Cooking
Time

30 minutes

YOU WILL NEED:

- 2 tablespoons olive oil (30 milliliters)
- 1 pound boneless, skinless chicken thighs, cubed (450 grams)
- 1 small onion, chopped
- 2 cloves garlic, minced
- 1 can artichoke hearts, drained and chopped (400 grams)
- 2 medium potatoes, diced
- 4 cups chicken broth (1 liter)
- 1/2 teaspoon dried oregano
- 1 teaspoon sea salt
- 1/2 teaspoon black pepper
- 1/2 cup heavy cream (120 milliliters)
- 1/4 cup grated Parmesan cheese

METHOD:

1. **Brown the Chicken:** Heat olive oil in a large pot over medium heat. Add chicken and cook for 6 minutes until browned.
2. **Sauté Vegetables:** Stir in onions, garlic, artichokes, and potatoes. Cook for 5 minutes until the potatoes begin to soften.
3. **Simmer the Chowder:** Pour in the chicken broth, oregano, salt, and pepper. Bring to a boil, reduce heat, and simmer for 15 minutes until potatoes are tender.
4. **Add Cream and Parmesan:** Stir in the heavy cream and Parmesan cheese. Cook for another 5 minutes before serving.

Nutritional information per serving: 450 calories, 30 grams protein, 20 grams fat, 40 grams carbohydrates

Expert TIP: This chowder has a bright, spring-like flavor thanks to the artichokes. Top with fresh parsley or chives for added freshness.

SPICED MOROCCAN CHICKEN STEW

Best season: Fall
Dairy-free, Gluten-free

Servings
6

Preparation Time
15 minutes

Cooking Time
1 hour

YOU WILL NEED:

- 2 tablespoons olive oil (30 milliliters)
- 1 pound boneless, skinless chicken thighs, cubed (450 grams)
- 1 large onion, diced
- 2 cloves garlic, minced
- 1 tablespoon ground cumin
- 1 teaspoon ground cinnamon
- 1 teaspoon ground coriander
- 1/2 teaspoon turmeric
- 1/4 teaspoon cayenne pepper
- 2 medium carrots, diced
- 1 large zucchini, chopped
- 1 can diced tomatoes (400 grams)
- 4 cups chicken broth (1 liter)
- 1/2 cup dried apricots, chopped (90 grams)
- 1/4 cup fresh cilantro, chopped

METHOD:

1. **Brown the Chicken:** Heat olive oil in a large pot over medium-high heat. Add chicken and brown on all sides, about 8 minutes. Remove and set aside.

2. **Sauté Vegetables and Spices:** Add onions and garlic to the pot and cook for 5 minutes. Stir in cumin, cinnamon, coriander, turmeric, and cayenne. Cook for 1 minute.

3. **Simmer the Stew:** Add carrots, zucchini, tomatoes, broth, and apricots. Return the chicken to the pot and bring to a boil. Reduce heat, cover, and simmer for 45 minutes.

4. **Finish and Serve:** Garnish with fresh cilantro before serving.

Nutritional information per serving: 410 calories, 26 grams protein, 12 grams fat, 45 grams carbohydrates

Expert TIP: The dried apricots add a subtle sweetness that contrasts with the warm spices, creating a rich, fragrant stew. Serve with couscous or rice.

CHICKEN AND WHITE BEAN CHILI

Best season: Winter
Gluten-free, Diabetic-friendly

Servings
4

Preparation Time
10 minutes

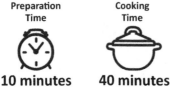
Cooking Time
40 minutes

YOU WILL NEED:

- 1 tablespoon olive oil (15 milliliters)
- 1 pound ground chicken (450 grams)
- 1 small onion, diced
- 2 cloves garlic, minced
- 1 can white beans, drained and rinsed (400 grams)
- 4 cups chicken broth (1 liter)
- 1 can diced green chiles (120 grams)
- 1 teaspoon ground cumin
- 1/2 teaspoon dried oregano
- 1 teaspoon sea salt
- 1/2 teaspoon black pepper
- 1/4 cup fresh cilantro, chopped

METHOD:

1. **Brown the Chicken:** Heat olive oil in a large pot. Add ground chicken and cook until browned, about 8 minutes.

2. **Add Aromatics and Spices:** Stir in onions, garlic, cumin, oregano, salt, and pepper. Cook for 5 minutes.

3. **Simmer the Chili:** Add white beans, chicken broth, and green chiles. Bring to a boil, reduce heat, and simmer for 25 minutes.

4. **Serve:** Garnish with fresh cilantro and serve with lime wedges or a dollop of sour cream.

Nutritional information per serving: 380 calories, 30 grams protein, 12 grams fat, 30 grams carbohydrates

Expert TIP: This white chili is a lighter alternative to traditional beef-based versions, offering a zesty, creamy flavor. Add diced avocado for an extra creamy texture.

CHICKEN TORTILLA SOUP

Best season: Fall
Gluten-free

Servings

6

Preparation Time

15 minutes

Cooking Time

35 minutes

YOU WILL NEED:

- 2 tablespoons olive oil (30 milliliters)
- 1 pound boneless, skinless chicken breasts, shredded (450 grams)
- 1 large onion, chopped
- 2 cloves garlic, minced
- 1 can diced tomatoes with green chiles (400 grams)
- 1 teaspoon ground cumin
- 1 teaspoon smoked paprika
- 1 teaspoon sea salt
- 1/2 teaspoon black pepper
- 6 cups chicken broth (1.5 liters)
- 1 cup frozen corn (150 grams)
- 1/2 cup black beans, rinsed and drained (120 grams)
- 1/4 cup fresh cilantro, chopped
- Tortilla strips for topping
- 1 avocado, sliced

METHOD:

1. **Sauté the Vegetables:** Heat olive oil in a large pot over medium heat. Add onion and garlic, and cook until softened, about 5 minutes.

2. **Simmer the Soup:** Add shredded chicken, diced tomatoes, cumin, smoked paprika, salt, pepper, and chicken broth. Bring to a boil, reduce heat, and simmer for 20 minutes.

3. **Add Corn and Beans:** Stir in frozen corn, black beans, and cilantro. Cook for an additional 5 minutes.

4. **Serve:** Ladle into bowls and top with crispy tortilla strips, avocado slices, and extra cilantro.

Nutritional information per serving: 360 calories, 28 grams protein, 12 grams fat, 30 grams carbohydrates

Expert TIP: For extra crunch, fry your own tortilla strips or buy pre-made ones to save time. A squeeze of lime adds a zesty finish!

GREEK LEMON CHICKEN SOUP (AVGOLEMONO)

Best season: Spring
Gluten-free, Low sodium

Servings
4

Preparation
Time
10 minutes

Cooking
Time
30 minutes

YOU WILL NEED:

- 1 pound boneless, skinless chicken thighs, shredded (450 grams)
- 6 cups chicken broth (1.5 liters)
- 1/2 cup orzo pasta (100 grams)
- 3 eggs
- 2 lemons, juiced
- 1 teaspoon sea salt
- 1/4 teaspoon black pepper
- 2 tablespoons fresh dill, chopped

METHOD:

1. **Cook Chicken and Orzo:** Bring chicken broth to a boil in a large pot. Add chicken thighs and cook for 10-12 minutes until tender. Remove chicken, shred, and return to the pot. Add orzo and cook until tender, about 8 minutes.

2. **Prepare the Egg-Lemon Mixture:** In a bowl, whisk together the eggs and lemon juice. Slowly add a ladle of hot broth to the mixture, whisking constantly to temper the eggs.

3. **Finish the Soup:** Slowly stir the egg-lemon mixture into the soup while whisking to avoid curdling. Season with salt, pepper, and dill.

4. **Serve:** Ladle into bowls and garnish with extra dill.

Nutritional information per serving: 350 calories, 28 grams protein, 10 grams fat, 30 grams carbohydrates

Expert TIP: This soup is silky and bright with a unique tang from the lemon. Serve with crusty bread for a complete meal.

CHICKEN, KALE, AND SWEET POTATO STEW

Best season: Winter
Gluten-free, Dairy-free

Servings
4

Preparation Time
10 minutes

Cooking Time
50 minutes

YOU WILL NEED:

- 1 tablespoon olive oil (15 milliliters)
- 1 pound boneless, skinless chicken breasts, cubed (450 grams)
- 1 large sweet potato, peeled and cubed
- 1 bunch kale, stems removed, chopped
- 1 small onion, diced
- 2 cloves garlic, minced
- 4 cups chicken broth (1 liter)
- 1 teaspoon smoked paprika
- 1/2 teaspoon ground cumin
- 1/2 teaspoon sea salt
- 1/4 teaspoon black pepper

METHOD:

1. **Brown the Chicken:** Heat olive oil in a large pot. Add cubed chicken and cook until browned, about 7 minutes. Remove and set aside.
2. **Sauté Vegetables:** Add onions, garlic, and sweet potatoes to the pot. Cook for 5 minutes, then stir in kale and cook until wilted, about 2 minutes.
3. **Simmer the Stew:** Pour in chicken broth, smoked paprika, cumin, salt, and pepper. Return the chicken to the pot and simmer for 30 minutes until the sweet potatoes are tender.
4. **Serve:** Adjust seasoning as needed and serve hot.

Nutritional information per serving: 400 calories, 32 grams protein, 10 grams fat, 40 grams carbohydrates

Expert TIP: The natural sweetness of the sweet potatoes pairs beautifully with the earthy kale and chicken. This stew is both hearty and nourishing.

CHICKEN AND QUINOA SOUP WITH AVOCADO

Best season: Spring
Gluten-free, Diabetic-friendly

Servings
4

Preparation Time
10 minutes

Cooking Time
30 minutes

YOU WILL NEED:

- 1 tablespoon olive oil (15 milliliters)
- 1 pound boneless, skinless chicken breasts, shredded (450 grams)
- 1 small onion, diced
- 2 cloves garlic, minced
- 1/2 cup quinoa, rinsed (100 grams)
- 6 cups chicken broth (1.5 liters)
- 1 teaspoon ground cumin
- 1 teaspoon sea salt
- 1/2 teaspoon black pepper
- 1 avocado, sliced
- 1/4 cup fresh cilantro, chopped

METHOD:

1. **Cook Chicken and Quinoa:** Heat olive oil in a large pot. Add onions and garlic, cooking for 5 minutes until softened. Add shredded chicken, quinoa, cumin, salt, and pepper. Pour in chicken broth and bring to a boil.
2. **Simmer the Soup:** Reduce heat and simmer for 20 minutes until the quinoa is tender.
3. **Serve:** Ladle into bowls and top with avocado slices and fresh cilantro.

Nutritional information per serving: 380 calories, 28 grams protein, 15 grams fat, 35 grams carbohydrates

Expert TIP: Quinoa adds a hearty texture to the soup, while the creamy avocado provides a rich contrast. This soup is perfect for a light, spring dinner.

TUSCAN CHICKEN AND WHITE BEAN STEW

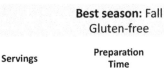

Best season: Fall
Gluten-free

Servings	Preparation Time	Cooking Time
4	15 minutes	40 minutes

YOU WILL NEED:

- 2 tablespoons olive oil (30 milliliters)
- 1 pound boneless, skinless chicken breasts, cubed (450 grams)
- 1 large onion, diced
- 2 cloves garlic, minced
- 1 can white beans, drained and rinsed (400 grams)
- 4 cups chicken broth (1 liter)
- 1 can diced tomatoes (400 grams)
- 1 teaspoon dried rosemary
- 1/2 teaspoon sea salt
- 1/4 teaspoon black pepper
- 2 cups spinach leaves (120 grams)
- 1 tablespoon balsamic vinegar

METHOD:

1. **Sauté the Chicken:** Heat olive oil in a large pot. Add cubed chicken and cook for 7 minutes until browned. Remove and set aside.

2. **Cook Vegetables:** In the same pot, sauté onions and garlic for 5 minutes.

3. **Simmer the Stew:** Stir in white beans, chicken broth, diced tomatoes, rosemary, salt, and pepper. Return the chicken to the pot and bring to a boil. Reduce heat and simmer for 25 minutes.

4. **Add Spinach and Balsamic:** Stir in spinach and balsamic vinegar just before serving.

Nutritional information per serving: 380 calories, 30 grams protein, 12 grams fat, 35 grams carbohydrates

Expert TIP: The balsamic vinegar adds a tangy depth to this hearty stew. Serve with crusty bread to soak up all the delicious flavors.

PERUVIAN CHICKEN STEW (AJI DE GALLINA)

Best season: Fall
Gluten-free

Servings	Preparation Time	Cooking Time
4	15 minutes	1 hour

YOU WILL NEED:

- 1 tablespoon olive oil (15 milliliters)
- 1 pound boneless, skinless chicken breasts, shredded (450 grams)
- 1 small onion, diced
- 2 cloves garlic, minced
- 1/2 cup evaporated milk (120 milliliters)
- 1/2 cup crushed walnuts (50 grams)
- 1/2 cup chicken broth (120 milliliters)
- 1 tablespoon aji amarillo paste (Peruvian yellow chili paste)
- 1 teaspoon sea salt
- 1/4 teaspoon black pepper
- 1/4 cup fresh parsley, chopped

METHOD:

1. **Cook Chicken:** In a large pot, heat olive oil over medium heat. Add shredded chicken, onion, and garlic. Cook for 10 minutes until softened.

2. **Make the Sauce:** Stir in evaporated milk, walnuts, chicken broth, aji amarillo paste, salt, and pepper. Bring to a simmer and cook for 30 minutes, stirring occasionally.

3. **Serve:** Garnish with fresh parsley before serving.

Nutritional information per serving: 450 calories, 30 grams protein, 20 grams fat, 35 grams carbohydrates

Expert TIP: Aji de Gallina is a classic Peruvian dish known for its creamy, slightly spicy sauce. Serve over rice for a complete meal. If you can't find Aji Amarillo paste, replace it with a blend of roasted yellow bell pepper and a pinch of cayenne pepper.

SPICY CHICKEN AND SAUSAGE GUMBO

Best season: Summer
Gluten-free

Servings	Preparation Time	Cooking Time

6	15 minutes	1 hour 30 minutes

YOU WILL NEED:

- 2 tablespoons vegetable oil (30 milliliters)
- 1 pound boneless, skinless chicken thighs, cubed (450 grams)
- 1/2 pound andouille sausage, sliced (225 grams)
- 1 small onion, diced
- 1 green bell pepper, diced
- 2 celery stalks, chopped
- 3 cloves garlic, minced
- 1/4 cup gluten-free flour (30 grams)
- 4 cups chicken broth (1 liter)
- 1 can diced tomatoes (400 grams)
- 1 teaspoon smoked paprika
- 1 teaspoon cayenne pepper
- 1/2 teaspoon sea salt
- 1/4 teaspoon black pepper
- 2 cups okra, sliced

METHOD:

1. **Brown Chicken and Sausage:** Heat vegetable oil in a large pot. Add chicken and sausage, cooking until browned, about 10 minutes. Remove and set aside.

2. **Make the Roux:** In the same pot, add gluten-free flour and stir constantly for 5 minutes until it turns golden brown.

3. **Sauté Vegetables:** Add onion, bell pepper, celery, and garlic. Cook for 5 minutes.

4. **Simmer Gumbo:** Stir in chicken broth, diced tomatoes, smoked paprika, cayenne, salt, pepper, and okra. Return the chicken and sausage to the pot. Bring to a boil, reduce heat, and simmer for 1 hour.

5. **Serve:** Garnish with fresh parsley or scallions.

Nutritional information per serving: 500 calories, 35 grams protein, 25 grams fat, 40 grams carbohydrates

Expert TIP: Gumbo is a classic Southern dish, and this gluten-free version still packs plenty of flavor. Serve over rice for a traditional experience.

Best season: Summer
Gluten-free, Dairy-free

Servings	Preparation Time	Cooking Time

4	10 minutes	45 minutes

YOU WILL NEED:

- 1 tablespoon olive oil (15 milliliters)
- 1 pound boneless, skinless chicken thighs, shredded (450 grams)
- 1 small onion, diced
- 2 cloves garlic, minced
- 4 cups chicken broth (1 liter)
- 1 can hominy, drained (400 grams)
- 1 cup tomatillo salsa (240 grams)
- 1 teaspoon ground cumin
- 1 teaspoon dried oregano
- 1/2 teaspoon sea salt
- 1/4 teaspoon black pepper
- 1/4 cup fresh cilantro, chopped
- 1 lime, cut into wedges

METHOD:

1. **Brown the Chicken:** Heat olive oil in a large pot. Add shredded chicken and cook for 5 minutes until browned. Remove and set aside.

2. **Cook Vegetables:** Stir in onions and garlic, cooking for 5 minutes.

3. **Simmer the Pozole:** Add chicken broth, hominy, tomatillo salsa, cumin, oregano, salt, and pepper. Return the chicken to the pot and bring to a boil. Reduce heat and simmer for 30 minutes.

4. **Serve:** Garnish with fresh cilantro and lime wedges before serving.

Nutritional information per serving: 380 calories, 28 grams protein, 12 grams fat, 35 grams carbohydrates

Expert TIP: This dish is a refreshing take on the traditional Mexican pozole, using tomatillo salsa to add a tangy flavor. Serve with shredded cabbage or radishes for extra crunch.

Best season: Summer
Gluten-free

Servings	Preparation Time	Cooking Time
4	10 minutes	35 minutes

YOU WILL NEED:

- 1 tablespoon olive oil (15 milliliters)
- 1 pound ground turkey (450 grams)
- 1 small onion, diced
- 2 cloves garlic, minced
- 3 ears fresh corn, kernels removed
- 1 medium zucchini, diced
- 4 cups chicken broth (1 liter)
- 1 teaspoon ground cumin
- 1/2 teaspoon sea salt
- 1/4 teaspoon black pepper
- 1/2 cup heavy cream (120 milliliters)
- 2 tablespoons fresh basil, chopped

METHOD:

1. **Brown the Turkey:** Heat olive oil in a large pot over medium heat. Add ground turkey and cook until browned, about 6-8 minutes.

2. **Cook Vegetables:** Stir in onions, garlic, corn kernels, and zucchini. Cook for 5 minutes until vegetables begin to soften.

3. **Simmer the Stew:** Add chicken broth, cumin, salt, and pepper. Bring to a boil, then reduce heat and simmer for 20 minutes.

4. **Finish and Serve:** Stir in the heavy cream and fresh basil just before serving.

Nutritional information per serving: 390 calories, 28 grams protein, 18 grams fat, 35 grams carbohydrates

Expert TIP: This stew celebrates fresh summer corn and zucchini, making it perfect for a late summer meal. Pair with a crisp salad for a light dinner.

TURKEY AND VEGETABLE CHOWDER

Best season: Winter
Diabetic-friendly

Servings

Preparation Time

Cooking Time

4

15 minutes

30 minutes

YOU WILL NEED:

- 1 tablespoon olive oil (15 milliliters)
- 1 pound ground turkey (450 grams)
- 1 small onion, diced
- 2 cloves garlic, minced
- 1 medium zucchini, diced
- 2 medium carrots, diced
- 2 medium potatoes, diced
- 4 cups chicken broth (1 liter)
- 1 teaspoon dried thyme
- 1/2 teaspoon sea salt
- 1/4 teaspoon black pepper
- 1 cup heavy cream (240 milliliters)

METHOD:

1. **Brown the Turkey:** Heat olive oil in a large pot. Add ground turkey and cook until browned, about 7-8 minutes.

2. **Cook Vegetables:** Stir in onions, garlic, zucchini, carrots, and potatoes. Cook for 5 minutes until vegetables begin to soften.

3. **Simmer the Chowder:** Add chicken broth, thyme, salt, and pepper. Bring to a boil, reduce heat, and simmer for 20 minutes until vegetables are tender.

4. **Add Cream:** Stir in heavy cream and cook for another 5 minutes before serving.

Nutritional information per serving: 420 calories, 28 grams protein, 22 grams fat, 35 grams carbohydrates

Expert TIP: This chowder is versatile and hearty—feel free to add other seasonal vegetables like corn or peas for extra flavor.

TURKEY, KALE, AND WHITE BEAN STEW

Best season: Fall
Diabetic-friendly, Low sodium

Servings
4

Preparation Time
10 minutes

Cooking Time
40 minutes

YOU WILL NEED:

- 1 tablespoon olive oil (15 milliliters)
- 1 pound ground turkey (450 grams)
- 1 small onion, diced
- 2 cloves garlic, minced
- 1 bunch kale, stems removed and chopped
- 1 can white beans, drained and rinsed (400 grams)
- 4 cups low-sodium chicken broth (1 liter)
- 1 teaspoon dried thyme
- 1/2 teaspoon sea salt
- 1/4 teaspoon black pepper
- 1/2 teaspoon red pepper flakes (optional)
- 2 tablespoons fresh parsley, chopped

METHOD:

1. **Brown the Turkey:** In a large pot, heat olive oil over medium heat. Add ground turkey and cook until browned, about 8 minutes.
2. **Cook Vegetables:** Stir in onions and garlic, and cook for 3 minutes. Add kale and cook until wilted, about 2 minutes.
3. **Simmer the Stew:** Stir in white beans, chicken broth, thyme, salt, pepper, and red pepper flakes (if using). Bring to a boil, reduce heat, and simmer for 25 minutes.
4. **Finish and Serve:** Garnish with fresh parsley before serving.

Nutritional information per serving: 310 calories, 28 grams protein, 12 grams fat, 25 grams carbohydrates

Expert TIP: For added richness, stir in a tablespoon of olive oil just before serving.

HEARTY TURKEY AND BARLEY SOUP

Best season: Winter
Gluten-free

Servings
6

Preparation Time
15 minutes

Cooking Time
1 hour

YOU WILL NEED:

- 2 tablespoons olive oil (30 milliliters)
- 1 pound cooked turkey, shredded (450 grams)
- 1 large carrot, diced
- 2 celery stalks, diced
- 1 small onion, chopped
- 1 cup pearl barley (200 grams)
- 6 cups turkey or chicken broth (1.5 liters)
- 1 teaspoon dried thyme
- 1 teaspoon sea salt
- 1/2 teaspoon black pepper
- 1 bay leaf
- 1/4 cup fresh parsley, chopped

METHOD:

1. **Sauté Vegetables:** In a large pot, heat olive oil over medium heat. Add carrots, celery, and onions, cooking for 5 minutes until softened.
2. **Simmer with Barley:** Stir in pearl barley, broth, thyme, salt, pepper, and bay leaf. Bring to a boil, then reduce heat and simmer for 40 minutes, or until the barley is tender.
3. **Add Turkey:** Stir in shredded turkey and cook for an additional 10 minutes until heated through. Garnish with fresh parsley before serving.

Nutritional information per serving: 380 calories, 25 grams protein, 14 grams fat, 40 grams carbohydrates

Expert TIP: This soup is even better the next day as the barley continues to absorb the flavors. Freeze any leftovers for a quick meal.

MAPLE-GLAZED TURKEY AND SWEET POTATO CHILI

Best season: Winter
Gluten-free

Servings	Preparation Time	Cooking Time
6	15 minutes	1 hour

YOU WILL NEED:

- 1 tablespoon olive oil (15 milliliters)
- 1 pound turkey breast, diced (450 grams)
- 1 large onion, diced
- 2 medium sweet potatoes, peeled and cubed
- 1 red bell pepper, diced
- 2 cloves garlic, minced
- 1 teaspoon ground cinnamon
- 1 teaspoon ground cumin
- 1/2 teaspoon smoked paprika
- 1/4 teaspoon chili flakes (optional)
- 3 tablespoons maple syrup (45 milliliters)
- 1 can diced tomatoes (400 grams)
- 2 cups chicken broth (500 milliliters)
- 1/2 teaspoon sea salt
- 1/4 teaspoon black pepper
- 1/4 cup fresh parsley, chopped

METHOD:

1. **Sear the Turkey:** In a large pot, heat olive oil over medium heat. Add the diced turkey and cook until browned, about 7-8 minutes. Remove and set aside.

2. **Cook vegetables and spices:** Add the onion, sweet potatoes, and red bell pepper to the pot, cooking for 5 minutes until slightly softened. Stir in garlic, cinnamon, cumin, smoked paprika, and chili flakes, cooking for another minute until fragrant.

3. **Add Maple Syrup and Simmer:** Stir in the maple syrup, diced tomatoes, chicken broth, sea salt, and black pepper. Return the turkey to the pot and simmer for 45 minutes, until the sweet potatoes are tender and the flavors have melded.

4. **Serve:** Garnish with fresh parsley and enjoy the sweet-spicy balance of flavors.

Nutritional information per serving: 410 calories, 28 grams protein, 12 grams fat, 45 grams carbohydrates

Expert TIP: The maple syrup adds a subtle sweetness that complements the savory spices and turkey. Serve with cornbread for an extra cozy winter meal.

SMOKY TURKEY AND BLACK BEAN STEW

Best season: Fall
Gluten-free, Dairy-free

Servings	Preparation Time	Cooking Time
4	15 minutes	40 minutes

YOU WILL NEED:

- 1 tablespoon olive oil (15 milliliters)
- 1 pound ground turkey (450 grams)
- 1 small onion, diced
- 3 cloves garlic, minced
- 1 teaspoon smoked paprika
- 1 teaspoon ground cumin
- 1/2 teaspoon chili powder
- 1 can diced tomatoes (400 grams)
- 2 cups chicken broth (500 milliliters)
- 1 can black beans, drained and rinsed (400 grams)
- 1 medium red bell pepper, diced
- 1 cup frozen corn (150 grams)
- 1/2 teaspoon sea salt
- 1/4 teaspoon black pepper
- 2 tablespoons fresh cilantro, chopped
- 1 lime, cut into wedges

METHOD:

1. **Brown the Turkey:** Heat olive oil in a large pot over medium heat. Add ground turkey and cook, breaking it apart, until browned, about 8 minutes.

2. **Cook vegetables and spices:** Stir in onion, garlic, smoked paprika, cumin, and chili powder. Cook for 5 minutes until onions are softened and fragrant.

3. **Simmer the Stew:** Add diced tomatoes, chicken broth, black beans, red bell pepper, corn, salt, and pepper. Bring to a boil, reduce heat, and simmer for 20 minutes until the flavors meld and vegetables are tender.

4. **Finish and Serve:** Stir in fresh cilantro and serve with lime wedges on the side for a zesty finish.

Nutritional information per serving: 380 calories, 30 grams protein, 12 grams fat, 40 grams carbohydrates

Expert TIP: The smoky paprika adds depth and warmth to the stew, while the lime brings brightness. Serve with tortilla chips for extra crunch!

LEMON CHICKEN ORZO SOUP

Best season: Spring
Diabetic-friendly

Servings	Preparation Time	Cooking Time
4	10 minutes	30 minutes

YOU WILL NEED:

- 1 tablespoon olive oil (15 milliliters)
- 1 pound boneless, skinless chicken breasts, cubed (450 grams)
- 1 large leek, thinly sliced
- 2 cloves garlic, minced
- 1 cup orzo pasta (200 grams)
- 4 cups chicken broth (1 liter)
- 1 cup spinach leaves (60 grams)
- 1/2 teaspoon dried oregano
- 1/2 teaspoon sea salt
- 1/4 teaspoon black pepper
- 1 lemon, zest and juice
- 2 tablespoons fresh parsley, chopped

METHOD:

1. **Sauté Chicken:** Heat olive oil in a large pot over medium heat. Add chicken and cook until browned, about 6 minutes. Remove from the pot and set aside.
2. **Cook Leeks and Garlic:** In the same pot, sauté the sliced leeks and garlic for 5 minutes until softened.
3. **Simmer Soup:** Add the orzo, chicken broth, oregano, salt, and pepper. Bring to a boil, then reduce heat and simmer for 10 minutes.
4. **Finish with Spinach and Lemon:** Stir in the cooked chicken, spinach, lemon zest, and juice. Simmer for another 5 minutes. Garnish with fresh parsley before serving.

Nutritional information per serving: 380 calories, 32 grams protein, 12 grams fat, 35 grams carbohydrates

Expert TIP: This soup is fresh and light, perfect for a spring lunch. For extra texture, add some toasted pine nuts before serving.

CHICKEN SOUP WITH ROASTED GARLIC AND SPINACH

Best season: Spring
Diabetic-friendly, Gluten-free

Servings	Preparation Time	Cooking Time
6	15 minutes	1 hour

YOU WILL NEED:

- 2 tablespoons olive oil
- 1 whole chicken breast, cubed
- 1 bulb of garlic, roasted and mashed
- 1 large onion, chopped
- 6 cups chicken broth
- 2 cups fresh spinach
- 1 teaspoon dried basil
- Salt and pepper to taste

METHOD:

1. **SRoast Garlic and Cook Chicken:** In a pot, heat olive oil over medium heat, add cubed chicken, and cook until browned. Stir in roasted garlic paste.
2. **Simmer with Spinach:** Add onion, chicken broth, and bring to a simmer. After 45 minutes, add spinach and basil, cooking until spinach is wilted. Season to taste.

FISH AND SEAFOOD SOUPS

FISHERMAN'S WINTER STEW

Best season: Winter
Gluten-free, Dairy-free

Servings

6

Preparation Time

20 minutes

Cooking Time

40 minutes

YOU WILL NEED:

- 2 tablespoons olive oil (30 milliliters)
- 1 large onion, diced
- 2 carrots, sliced
- 2 celery stalks, diced
- 3 cloves garlic, minced
- 1 pound firm white fish fillets (such as cod, halibut, or sea bass), cut into chunks (450 grams)
- 1 can diced tomatoes (400 grams)
- 4 cups fish stock or vegetable broth (1 liter)
- 1 teaspoon smoked paprika
- 1 teaspoon sea salt
- 1/2 teaspoon black pepper
- 1 bay leaf
- 1/4 cup fresh parsley, chopped

METHOD:

1. **Sauté Vegetables:** Heat olive oil in a large pot over medium heat. Add the onion, carrots, celery, and garlic. Cook for 8-10 minutes until the vegetables are softened.

2. **Simmer the Broth:** Add diced tomatoes, fish stock, smoked paprika, bay leaf, salt, and pepper. Bring to a boil, reduce heat, and simmer for 25 minutes.

3. **Add the Fish:** Stir in the fish chunks and simmer for another 10 minutes until the fish is cooked through and flakes easily.

4. **Serve:** Remove the bay leaf, garnish with fresh parsley, and serve hot with a squeeze of lemon.

Nutritional information per serving: 300 calories, 28 grams protein, 12 grams fat, 20 grams carbohydrates

Expert TIP: The smoked paprika adds a subtle warmth, while the fish stays tender and flavorful. Serve with roasted vegetables or a side salad.

SMOKY FISH AND LENTIL STEW

Best season: Winter
Gluten-free, Dairy-free

Servings

4

Preparation
Time

15 minutes

Cooking
Time

35 minutes

YOU WILL NEED:

- 1 tablespoon olive oil (15 milliliters)
- 1 small onion, diced
- 2 cloves garlic, minced
- 1 small carrot, diced
- 1 cup dried green lentils (200 grams)
- 1 can diced tomatoes (400 grams)
- 4 cups fish broth (1 liter)
- 1 pound white fish fillets (such as cod or haddock), cut into chunks (450 grams)
- 1 teaspoon smoked paprika
- 1 teaspoon ground cumin
- 1/2 teaspoon sea salt
- 1/4 teaspoon black pepper
- 2 tablespoons fresh parsley, chopped

METHOD:

1. **Sauté Aromatics:** Heat olive oil in a large pot over medium heat. Add diced onion, garlic, and carrots, and cook for 5 minutes until softened.

2. **Simmer the Lentils:** Add lentils, diced tomatoes, fish broth, smoked paprika, cumin, salt, and pepper. Bring to a boil, reduce heat, and simmer for 20-25 minutes until the lentils are tender.

3. **Add Fish:** Gently stir in the fish chunks and simmer for another 8-10 minutes until the fish is cooked through and flakes easily.

4. **Serve:** Garnish with fresh parsley and serve hot, with a wedge of lemon for extra brightness.

Nutritional information per serving: 360 calories, 32 grams protein, 10 grams fat, 40 grams carbohydrates

Expert TIP: The smoky flavor from the paprika gives the stew a comforting depth, while the lentils add heartiness and texture. This stew is warming and nutritious, perfect for winter evenings.

HERBED FISH STEW WITH POTATOES

Best season: Winter
Gluten-free, Dairy-free

Servings

4

Preparation
Time

15 minutes

Cooking
Time

40 minutes

YOU WILL NEED:

- 2 tablespoons olive oil (30 milliliters)
- 1 large onion, diced
- 3 cloves garlic, minced
- 1 large carrot, sliced
- 3 medium Yukon Gold potatoes, cubed
- 1 teaspoon dried thyme
- 1 teaspoon dried oregano
- 4 cups fish or vegetable broth (1 liter)
- 1 can diced tomatoes (400 grams)
- 1 cup dry white wine (240 milliliters)
- 1 pound firm white fish fillets (such as cod or haddock), cut into chunks (450 grams)
- 1 teaspoon sea salt
- 1/2 teaspoon black pepper
- 1 tablespoon lemon juice
- 1/4 cup fresh parsley, chopped

METHOD:

1. **Sauté the Vegetables:** Heat olive oil in a large pot over medium heat. Add the diced onion, garlic, and sliced carrot. Cook for 5 minutes until the onion softens.

2. **Add the Potatoes and Herbs:** Stir in the cubed potatoes, thyme, and oregano. Sauté for another 2 minutes, allowing the potatoes to start absorbing the flavors.

3. **Simmer with Broth and Wine:** Add the broth, diced tomatoes, and white wine to the pot. Bring to a boil, reduce heat, and simmer for 20-25 minutes, or until the potatoes are tender.

4. **Add the Fish:** Gently add the fish chunks, sea salt, and black pepper to the stew. Simmer for another 7-10 minutes, or until the fish is cooked through and flakes easily.

5. **Finish and Serve:** Stir in the lemon juice and garnish with fresh parsley. Serve hot with crusty bread or over rice.

Nutritional information per serving: 400 calories, 30 grams protein, 12 grams fat, 35 grams carbohydrates

Expert TIP: The combination of fish, herbs, and potatoes makes this stew comforting and hearty. Add a pinch of red pepper flakes if you want a bit of heat!

SALMON AND LEEK CHOWDER

Best season: Winter
Gluten-free

Servings

4

Preparation
Time

10 minutes

Cooking
Time

25 minutes

YOU WILL NEED:

- 1 tablespoon unsalted butter (15 grams)
- 1 pound skinless salmon fillets, cubed (450 grams)
- 1 large leek, thinly sliced
- 2 medium potatoes, diced
- 1 clove garlic, minced
- 4 cups vegetable broth (1 liter)
- 1 cup heavy cream (240 milliliters)
- 1 teaspoon dried dill
- 1/2 teaspoon sea salt
- 1/4 teaspoon black pepper
- 1 tablespoon fresh chives, chopped

METHOD:

1. **Cook the Leeks:** In a large pot, melt butter over medium heat. Add sliced leeks and garlic, cooking for 5 minutes until softened.
2. **Simmer Potatoes:** Stir in diced potatoes and vegetable broth. Bring to a boil, reduce heat, and simmer for 15 minutes until the potatoes are tender.
3. **Add Salmon and Cream:** Stir in cubed salmon, heavy cream, dill, salt, and pepper. Cook for an additional 5-7 minutes until the salmon is just cooked through.
4. **Serve:** Garnish with fresh chives before serving.

Nutritional information per serving: 420 calories, 30 grams protein, 18 grams fat, 35 grams carbohydrates

Expert TIP: The mild flavor of leeks pairs beautifully with rich salmon, and the cream creates a velvety texture. For extra depth, add a splash of dry white wine.

MISO SALMON AND NOODLE SOUP

Best season: Winter
Gluten-free

Servings

4

Preparation Time

10 minutes

Cooking Time

20 minutes

YOU WILL NEED:

- 1 tablespoon sesame oil (15 milliliters)
- 1 pound salmon fillets, skin removed (450 grams)
- 1 small onion, thinly sliced
- 3 cloves garlic, minced
- 1 tablespoon fresh ginger, grated
- 6 cups chicken broth (1.5 liters)
- 2 tablespoons white miso paste
- 1 tablespoon soy sauce (gluten-free)
- 2 cups cooked rice noodles (200 grams)
- 1 cup baby spinach
- 1 teaspoon sea salt
- 1/4 teaspoon black pepper
- 1/4 cup green onions, chopped

METHOD:

1. **Sauté Aromatics:** Heat sesame oil in a large pot. Add onion, garlic, and ginger, cooking for 5 minutes until fragrant.

2. **Simmer the Broth:** Stir in chicken broth, miso paste, and soy sauce. Bring to a boil, reduce heat, and simmer for 10 minutes.

3. **Add Salmon and Spinach:** Stir in cubed salmon and baby spinach. Simmer for 5-7 minutes until the salmon is cooked through.

4. **Serve with Noodles:** Ladle over cooked rice noodles and garnish with green onions.

Nutritional information per serving: 380 calories, 32 grams protein, 12 grams fat, 40 grams carbohydrates

Expert TIP: The miso paste adds an umami depth to the broth, while the noodles make it a filling meal. For extra heat, add a drizzle of chili oil.

Best season: Winter
Gluten-free, Dairy-free

YOU WILL NEED:

Servings

4

Preparation Time

15 minutes

Cooking Time

35 minutes

- 2 tablespoons olive oil (30 milliliters)
- 1 small onion, diced
- 2 cloves garlic, minced
- 1 teaspoon ground cumin
- 1/2 teaspoon smoked paprika
- 1 can diced tomatoes (400 grams)
- 1 can chickpeas, drained and rinsed (400 grams)
- 4 cups vegetable or fish broth (1 liter)
- 1/2 cup dry white wine (120 milliliters)
- 1 pound cod fillets, cut into chunks (450 grams)
- 1 teaspoon sea salt
- 1/2 teaspoon black pepper
- 1 tablespoon lemon juice
- 1/4 cup fresh cilantro, chopped

METHOD:

1. **Sauté Aromatics:** Heat olive oil in a large pot over medium heat. Add the diced onion and garlic, cooking for 5 minutes until softened.

2. **Add Spices:** Stir in the ground cumin and smoked paprika, cooking for 1 minute to release their flavors.

3. **Simmer with Tomatoes and Chickpeas:** Add the diced tomatoes, chickpeas, vegetable broth, and white wine. Bring the mixture to a boil, then reduce heat and simmer for 20 minutes to allow the flavors to blend.

4. **Add the Cod:** Gently stir in the cod chunks, sea salt, and black pepper. Simmer for an additional 7-10 minutes until the cod is cooked through and flakes easily.

5. **Finish and Serve:** Stir in the lemon juice and garnish with fresh cilantro. Serve hot with a side of crusty bread or rice.

Nutritional information per serving: 380 calories, 30 grams protein, 12 grams fat, 35 grams carbohydrates

Expert TIP: The chickpeas add a hearty texture and richness to this stew, while the spices give it a warm, smoky flavor. Squeeze some extra lemon juice over the top for a fresh, zesty finish.

HEARTY COD AND CHICKPEA STEW

Best season: Winter
Gluten-free

YOU WILL NEED:

Servings

4

Preparation Time

15 minutes

Cooking Time

25 minutes

- 2 tablespoons unsalted butter (30 grams)
- 1 small onion, diced
- 2 cloves garlic, minced
- 3 medium potatoes, diced
- 1 cup smoked salmon, shredded (150 grams)
- 4 cups vegetable broth (1 liter)
- 1 cup heavy cream (240 milliliters)
- 1 teaspoon dried thyme
- 1 teaspoon sea salt
- 1/2 teaspoon black pepper
- 1 tablespoon fresh dill, chopped

METHOD:

1. **Sauté the Vegetables:** Melt butter in a large pot over medium heat. Add the onion and garlic and cook until softened, about 5 minutes.

2. **Simmer Potatoes:** Stir in the diced potatoes, vegetable broth, thyme, salt, and pepper. Bring to a boil, reduce heat, and simmer for 15 minutes until the potatoes are tender.

3. **Add Smoked Salmon and Cream:** Stir in the smoked salmon and heavy cream. Simmer for another 5 minutes, stirring occasionally.

4. **Serve:** Garnish with fresh dill and serve with crusty bread.

Nutritional information per serving: 400 calories, 22 grams protein, 22 grams fat, 35 grams carbohydrates

Expert TIP: The smoky flavor from the salmon gives the chowder depth and richness, making it perfect for a cold winter evening.

CORN AND COD CHOWDER

Best season: Summer
Gluten-free

Servings	Preparation Time	Cooking Time
4	10 minutes	25 minutes

YOU WILL NEED:

- 2 tablespoons butter (30 grams)
- 1 small onion, diced
- 2 medium potatoes, diced
- 1 cup fresh corn kernels (150 grams)
- 1 pound cod fillets, cubed (450 grams)
- 4 cups chicken broth (1 liter)
- 1 cup heavy cream (240 milliliters)
- 1 teaspoon smoked paprika
- 1 teaspoon sea salt
- 1/2 teaspoon black pepper
- 2 tablespoons fresh parsley, chopped

METHOD:

1. **Sauté Onions and Potatoes:** Melt butter in a large pot over medium heat. Add diced onion and potatoes, cooking for 5 minutes until softened.

2. **Simmer with Corn and Broth:** Stir in fresh corn kernels, chicken broth, smoked paprika, salt, and pepper. Bring to a boil, reduce heat, and simmer for 15 minutes until the potatoes are tender.

3. **Add Cod and Cream:** Stir in the cubed cod and heavy cream, and simmer for another 5-7 minutes until the fish is cooked through.

4. **Serve:** Garnish with fresh parsley before serving.

Nutritional information per serving: 410 calories, 28 grams protein, 22 grams fat, 30 grams carbohydrates

Expert TIP: The sweetness of the corn contrasts beautifully with the mild cod, and the cream adds a rich finish to this summer chowder.

COCONUT FISH AND SWEET POTATO STEW

Best season: Summer
Gluten-free, Dairy-free

Servings	Preparation Time	Cooking Time
4	15 minutes	30 minutes

YOU WILL NEED:

- 1 tablespoon coconut oil (15 milliliters)
- 1 pound white fish fillets (such as halibut or snapper), cubed (450 grams)
- 1 medium sweet potato, peeled and cubed
- 1 small onion, diced
- 2 cloves garlic, minced
- 1 teaspoon ground turmeric
- 1 teaspoon ground cumin
- 1 can coconut milk (400 milliliters)
- 4 cups vegetable broth (1 liter)
- 1 teaspoon sea salt
- 1/2 teaspoon black pepper
- 1 tablespoon fresh cilantro, chopped

METHOD:

1. **Sauté the Vegetables:** In a large pot, heat coconut oil over medium heat. Add onion and garlic, and sauté for 5 minutes until softened.

2. **Simmer with Sweet Potatoes:** Stir in sweet potatoes, turmeric, cumin, vegetable broth, salt, and pepper. Bring to a boil, reduce heat, and simmer for 15 minutes until the sweet potatoes are tender.

3. **Add Fish and Coconut Milk:** Stir in the cubed fish and coconut milk, and simmer for another 10 minutes until the fish is cooked through.

4. **Serve:** Garnish with fresh cilantro and serve with lime wedges for a citrusy finish.

Nutritional information per serving: 380 calories, 30 grams protein, 18 grams fat, 30 grams carbohydrates

Expert TIP: The rich coconut milk adds a creamy texture and complements the sweetness of the sweet potatoes, creating a satisfying summer stew.

CLASSIC CIOPPINO (SEAFOOD STEW)

Best season: Summer
Gluten-free, Dairy-free

Servings

6

Preparation Time

20 minutes

Cooking Time

45 minutes

YOU WILL NEED:

- 2 tablespoons olive oil (30 milliliters)
- 1 large onion, finely chopped
- 4 cloves garlic, minced
- 1 fennel bulb, thinly sliced
- 1 teaspoon crushed red pepper flakes (optional for heat)
- 1 teaspoon dried oregano
- 1 bay leaf
- 1 cup dry white wine (240 milliliters)
- 1 can (28 ounces/800 grams) diced tomatoes with juices
- 4 cups seafood or fish stock (1 liter)
- 1/2 cup tomato paste (120 grams)
- 1 pound firm white fish (such as cod, halibut, or sea bass), cut into chunks (450 grams)
- 1 pound mussels, cleaned and de-bearded (450 grams)
- 1/2 pound large shrimp, peeled and deveined (225 grams)
- 1/2 pound scallops (225 grams)
- 1/2 pound squid, sliced into rings (225 grams)
- 1/4 cup fresh parsley, chopped
- 1/4 cup fresh basil, chopped
- Sea salt and black pepper to taste
- Lemon wedges, for serving
- Crusty bread, for serving (optional)

METHOD:

1. **Sauté Aromatics:** Heat olive oil in a large, deep pot over medium heat. Add chopped onion, garlic, and sliced fennel. Cook for 8-10 minutes until the vegetables soften and become fragrant.

2. **Add Seasonings and Wine:** Stir in the crushed red pepper flakes, dried oregano, and bay leaf. Pour in the white wine, and simmer for 3-4 minutes until the wine reduces slightly.

3. **Simmer with Tomatoes and Stock:** Add the diced tomatoes, tomato paste, and seafood stock. Bring to a simmer, cover, and cook for 20-25 minutes to let the flavors meld together.

4. **Add Seafood:** Stir in the fish chunks and squid, allowing them to cook for 5 minutes. Then add the shrimp, mussels, and scallops, and cook for an additional 5-7 minutes, or until the shrimp turn pink and the mussels open. Discard any mussels that do not open.

5. **Finish and Serve:** Season the cioppino with sea salt and black pepper to taste. Stir in fresh parsley and basil before serving. Serve hot with lemon wedges on the side and crusty bread for dipping if desired.

Nutritional information per serving: 400 calories, 38 grams protein, 14 grams fat, 20 grams carbohydrates

Expert TIP: Cioppino is even better the next day, as the flavors deepen with time. You can easily adjust the mix of seafood depending on availability—add clams, lobster, or crab for an extra-luxurious version.

SEAFOOD CHOWDER WITH CLAMS, SHRIMP, AND CRAB

Best season: Winter
Gluten-free

Servings

6

Preparation Time

15 minutes

Cooking Time

40 minutes

YOU WILL NEED:

- 4 slices bacon, chopped
- 1 small onion, diced
- 2 cloves garlic, minced
- 2 medium potatoes, diced
- 1 cup fresh clams, cleaned
- 1 cup large shrimp, peeled and deveined (150 grams)
- 1/2 cup crab meat (75 grams)
- 4 cups seafood broth (1 liter)
- 1 cup heavy cream (240 milliliters)
- 1 teaspoon sea salt
- 1/2 teaspoon black pepper
- 1 teaspoon fresh thyme leaves
- 2 tablespoons fresh parsley, chopped

METHOD:

1. **Cook the Bacon:** In a large pot, cook bacon over medium heat until crispy, about 5 minutes. Remove and set aside, leaving the drippings in the pot.
2. **Sauté Vegetables:** Add onion, garlic, and diced potatoes to the pot. Cook for 5 minutes until softened.
3. **Simmer the Broth:** Stir in seafood broth, thyme, salt, and pepper. Bring to a boil, reduce heat, and simmer for 20 minutes until the potatoes are tender.
4. **Add Seafood and Cream:** Stir in clams, shrimp, crab meat, and heavy cream. Simmer for an additional 5-7 minutes until the seafood is cooked.
5. **Serve:** Garnish with bacon and fresh parsley before serving.

Nutritional information per serving: 450 calories, 30 grams protein, 22 grams fat, 30 grams carbohydrates

Expert TIP: The trio of seafood adds a luxurious touch to this creamy chowder. Serve with oyster crackers for a true coastal experience.

CAJUN SHRIMP AND CORN CHOWDER

Best season: Winter
Gluten-free

Servings

6

Preparation Time

15 minutes

Cooking Time

30 minutes

YOU WILL NEED:

- 1 tablespoon olive oil (15 milliliters)
- 1 pound large shrimp, peeled and deveined (450 grams)
- 1 small onion, diced
- 2 cloves garlic, minced
- 2 medium potatoes, diced
- 2 cups fresh corn kernels (300 grams)
- 4 cups chicken or seafood broth (1 liter)
- 1 teaspoon Cajun seasoning
- 1/2 teaspoon smoked paprika
- 1/2 teaspoon sea salt
- 1/4 teaspoon black pepper
- 1 cup coconut milk (240 milliliters)
- 2 tablespoons fresh parsley, chopped

METHOD:

1. **Sauté Shrimp:** Heat olive oil in a large pot over medium heat. Add the shrimp and cook for 2-3 minutes until just pink. Remove and set aside.
2. **Cook Vegetables:** Add onions, garlic, and diced potatoes to the pot. Cook for 5 minutes until softened. Stir in the fresh corn kernels, Cajun seasoning, smoked paprika, sea salt, and black pepper.
3. **Simmer with Broth:** Pour in the broth and bring to a boil. Reduce heat and simmer for 15 minutes until the potatoes are tender.
4. **Add Coconut Milk and Shrimp:** Stir in coconut milk and return the shrimp to the pot. Cook for an additional 5 minutes. Garnish with fresh parsley before serving.

Nutritional information per serving: 350 calories, 28 grams protein, 14 grams fat, 30 grams carbohydrates

Expert TIP: The Cajun seasoning adds a spicy kick, balanced by the sweetness of the corn and coconut milk. Serve with crusty bread for a satisfying meal.

SHRIMP AND RED LENTIL SOUP

Best season: Fall
Gluten-free, Dairy-free

Servings	Preparation Time	Cooking Time
4	10 minutes	25 minutes

YOU WILL NEED:

- 1 tablespoon olive oil (15 milliliters)
- 1 pound large shrimp, peeled and deveined (450 grams)
- 1 small onion, diced
- 2 cloves garlic, minced
- 1 cup red lentils (200 grams)
- 1 can diced tomatoes (400 grams)
- 4 cups vegetable broth (1 liter)
- 1 teaspoon ground cumin
- 1/2 teaspoon ground turmeric
- 1 teaspoon sea salt
- 1/4 teaspoon black pepper
- 1 tablespoon lemon juice
- 2 tablespoons fresh cilantro, chopped

METHOD:

1. **Sauté the Shrimp:** Heat olive oil in a large pot. Add shrimp and cook for 2-3 minutes until just pink. Remove and set aside.

2. **Sauté the Aromatics:** In the same pot, add onion, garlic, cumin, and turmeric. Cook for 5 minutes until softened.

3. **Simmer the Lentils:** Stir in red lentils, diced tomatoes, vegetable broth, salt, and pepper. Bring to a boil, reduce heat, and simmer for 15 minutes until the lentils are tender.

4. **Serve with Shrimp:** Stir in cooked shrimp and lemon juice. Garnish with fresh cilantro before serving.

Nutritional information per serving: 380 calories, 32 grams protein, 8 grams fat, 45 grams carbohydrates

Expert TIP: The red lentils give this soup a creamy texture while the shrimp add a fresh, ocean flavor. Serve with naan bread or pita for a full meal.

SEAFOOD GUMBO WITH ANDOUILLE SAUSAGE

Best season: Fall
Gluten-free

Servings

Preparation Time

Cooking Time

6   **20 minutes**   **1 hour**

YOU WILL NEED:

- 1/4 cup olive oil (60 milliliters)
- 1/4 cup gluten-free flour (30 grams)
- 1 pound large shrimp, peeled and deveined (450 grams)
- 1/2 pound crab meat (225 grams)
- 1/2 pound andouille sausage, sliced (225 grams)
- 1 small onion, diced
- 1 green bell pepper, diced
- 2 celery stalks, chopped
- 3 cloves garlic, minced
- 6 cups seafood broth (1.5 liters)
- 1 can diced tomatoes (400 grams)
- 1 teaspoon Cajun seasoning
- 1 bay leaf
- 1 teaspoon sea salt
- 1/2 teaspoon black pepper
- 2 tablespoons fresh parsley, chopped

METHOD:

1. **Make the Roux:** In a large pot, heat olive oil and gluten-free flour over medium heat, whisking constantly for 5-7 minutes until the mixture turns golden brown.

2. **Cook Vegetables and Sausage:** Stir in the onion, green bell pepper, celery, garlic, and andouille sausage. Cook for 5 minutes until softened.

3. **Simmer the Gumbo:** Add seafood broth, diced tomatoes, Cajun seasoning, bay leaf, salt, and pepper. Bring to a boil, reduce heat, and simmer for 45 minutes.

4. **Add Seafood:** Stir in shrimp and crab meat, and cook for an additional 5 minutes until the shrimp are pink. Garnish with parsley before serving.

Nutritional information per serving: 450 calories, 30 grams protein, 20 grams fat, 35 grams carbohydrates

Expert TIP: This rich gumbo is full of flavor, thanks to the smoky andouille sausage and Cajun spices. Serve over rice for a heartier meal.

NEW ENGLAND CLAM CHOWDER

Best season: Fall
Gluten-free

Servings	Preparation Time	Cooking Time
4	15 minutes	35 minutes

YOU WILL NEED:

- 4 slices bacon, chopped
- 1 small onion, diced
- 2 cloves garlic, minced
- 3 medium potatoes, diced
- 2 cans chopped clams with juice (300 grams each)
- 4 cups clam juice (1 liter)
- 1 cup heavy cream (240 milliliters)
- 1 teaspoon fresh thyme leaves
- 1 teaspoon sea salt
- 1/2 teaspoon black pepper
- 1 bay leaf
- 2 tablespoons fresh parsley, chopped

METHOD:

1. **Cook Bacon:** In a large pot, cook bacon over medium heat until crispy, about 5 minutes. Remove and set aside, leaving the drippings in the pot.
2. **Sauté Onions and Garlic:** Add onions and garlic to the pot, cooking for 3 minutes until softened.
3. **Simmer with Potatoes:** Stir in diced potatoes, clam juice, thyme, salt, pepper, and the bay leaf. Bring to a boil, reduce heat, and simmer for 20 minutes until potatoes are tender.
4. **Add Clams and Cream:** Stir in chopped clams, heavy cream, and cooked bacon. Simmer for another 5 minutes. Garnish with fresh parsley before serving.

Nutritional information per serving: 480 calories, 24 grams protein, 28 grams fat, 35 grams carbohydrates

Expert TIP: This chowder is classic New England comfort food. Serve with oyster crackers or a loaf of sourdough for an authentic experience.

CLAM AND SAUSAGE STEW

Best season: Summer
Gluten-free, Dairy-free

Servings	Preparation Time	Cooking Time
4	10 minutes	25 minutes

YOU WILL NEED:

- 1 tablespoon olive oil (15 milliliters)
- 1 pound fresh clams, cleaned (450 grams)
- 1/2 pound chorizo sausage, sliced (225 grams)
- 1 small onion, diced
- 2 cloves garlic, minced
- 1 can diced tomatoes (400 grams)
- 4 cups vegetable broth (1 liter)
- 1/2 teaspoon crushed red pepper flakes
- 1 teaspoon sea salt
- 1/4 teaspoon black pepper
- 1/4 cup fresh parsley, chopped

METHOD:

1. **Cook the Chorizo:** In a large pot, heat olive oil over medium heat. Add sliced chorizo and cook for 5 minutes until browned.
2. **Add Vegetables and Broth:** Stir in diced onion, garlic, diced tomatoes, red pepper flakes, salt, and pepper. Pour in the vegetable broth and bring to a boil.
3. **Add Clams:** Stir in clams, cover, and cook for 10-12 minutes until the clams open.
4. **Serve:** Garnish with fresh parsley and serve with crusty bread to soak up the flavorful broth.

Nutritional information per serving: 410 calories, 28 grams protein, 20 grams fat, 25 grams carbohydrates

Expert TIP: The smoky chorizo and briny clams make for an irresistible combination. For a touch of brightness, squeeze lemon juice over the stew before serving.

SCALLOP AND FENNEL STEW

Best season: Winter
Gluten-free

Servings

Preparation Time

Cooking Time

4　**10 minutes**　**30 minutes**

YOU WILL NEED:

- 1 tablespoon olive oil (15 milliliters)
- 1 pound sea scallops (450 grams)
- 1 large fennel bulb, thinly sliced
- 1 small onion, diced
- 2 cloves garlic, minced
- 1 can diced tomatoes (400 grams)
- 4 cups seafood broth (1 liter)
- 1 teaspoon fennel seeds, crushed
- 1/2 teaspoon sea salt
- 1/4 teaspoon black pepper
- 1 tablespoon lemon juice
- 2 tablespoons fresh dill, chopped

METHOD:

1. **Sauté the Fennel:** Heat olive oil in a large pot. Add sliced fennel, onion, and garlic, cooking for 5 minutes until softened.

2. **Simmer the Stew:** Stir in diced tomatoes, seafood broth, fennel seeds, salt, and pepper. Bring to a boil, reduce heat, and simmer for 20 minutes.

3. **Add Scallops:** Stir in the scallops and cook for an additional 5-7 minutes until they are opaque and tender.

4. **Serve:** Stir in lemon juice and garnish with fresh dill before serving.

Nutritional information per serving: 370 calories, 30 grams protein, 10 grams fat, 30 grams carbohydrates

Expert TIP: The fresh fennel and scallops create a light, flavorful dish, perfect for a cozy winter evening. Serve with a crisp white wine for an elegant pairing.

LOBSTER BISQUE WITH SAFFRON

Best season: Fall
Gluten-free

Servings	Preparation Time	Cooking Time
4	20 minutes	45 minutes

YOU WILL NEED:

- 2 lobster tails, cooked and chopped (300 grams)
- 2 tablespoons butter (30 grams)
- 1 small onion, diced
- 2 cloves garlic, minced
- 1 carrot, chopped
- 1 celery stalk, chopped
- 1 tablespoon tomato paste
- 1 teaspoon saffron threads
- 4 cups seafood broth (1 liter)
- 1 cup heavy cream (240 milliliters)
- 1 teaspoon sea salt
- 1/4 teaspoon black pepper
- 1 tablespoon fresh tarragon, chopped

METHOD:

1. **Sauté Vegetables:** In a large pot, melt butter over medium heat. Add onion, garlic, carrot, and celery, cooking for 5 minutes until softened.

2. **Add Tomato Paste and Saffron:** Stir in the tomato paste and saffron threads, cooking for another 2 minutes.

3. **Simmer the Bisque:** Add seafood broth, salt, and pepper. Bring to a boil, reduce heat, and simmer for 30 minutes.

4. **Blend and Add Lobster:** Use an immersion blender to purée the bisque until smooth. Stir in the chopped lobster and heavy cream. Simmer for 5 minutes.

5. **Serve:** Garnish with fresh tarragon before serving.

Nutritional information per serving: 480 calories, 28 grams protein, 28 grams fat, 20 grams carbohydrates

Expert TIP: The saffron gives this lobster bisque a unique and fragrant flavor. Serve with a glass of white wine for an elegant dinner.

LOBSTER AND ASPARAGUS BISQUE

Best season: Spring
Gluten-free

Servings

4

Preparation
Time

20 minutes

Cooking
Time

30 minutes

YOU WILL NEED:

- 2 lobster tails, cooked and chopped (300 grams)
- 1 tablespoon butter (15 grams)
- 1 small onion, diced
- 2 cloves garlic, minced
- 1 bunch asparagus, chopped (200 grams)
- 4 cups seafood broth (1 liter)
- 1/2 cup heavy cream (120 milliliters)
- 1 teaspoon smoked paprika
- 1 teaspoon sea salt
- 1/4 teaspoon black pepper
- 1 tablespoon lemon juice
- 2 tablespoons fresh chives, chopped

METHOD:

1. **Sauté the Vegetables:** In a large pot, melt butter over medium heat. Add onion, garlic, and asparagus, cooking for 5 minutes until softened.

2. **Simmer the Bisque:** Add seafood broth, smoked paprika, salt, and pepper. Bring to a boil, reduce heat, and simmer for 15 minutes.

3. **Blend and Add Lobster:** Use an immersion blender to purée the soup until smooth. Stir in heavy cream, lobster meat, and lemon juice. Simmer for 5 minutes.

4. **Serve:** Garnish with fresh chives before serving.

Nutritional information per serving: 440 calories, 28 grams protein, 20 grams fat, 30 grams carbohydrates

Expert TIP: The lobster and asparagus create a luxurious bisque with a light, fresh flavor. Serve with a side salad for an elegant springtime meal.

SPICY TOMATO FISH STEW

Best season: Fall
Gluten-free, Dairy-free

Servings

4

Preparation
Time

15 minutes

Cooking
Time

35 minutes

YOU WILL NEED:

- 1 tablespoon olive oil (15 milliliters)
- 1 pound white fish fillets (such as cod or tilapia), cubed (450 grams)
- 1 small onion, diced
- 3 cloves garlic, minced
- 1 red bell pepper, chopped
- 1 can diced tomatoes (400 grams)
- 4 cups vegetable broth (1 liter)
- 1 teaspoon ground cumin
- 1/2 teaspoon crushed red pepper flakes
- 1 teaspoon smoked paprika
- 1 teaspoon sea salt
- 1/4 cup fresh cilantro, chopped

METHOD:

1. **Sauté the Aromatics:** Heat olive oil in a large pot over medium heat. Add onion, garlic, and bell pepper, and sauté for 5 minutes until softened.

2. **Simmer the Broth:** Stir in diced tomatoes, vegetable broth, cumin, crushed red pepper flakes, smoked paprika, and sea salt. Bring to a boil, reduce heat, and simmer for 20 minutes.

3. **Add the Fish:** Stir in the cubed white fish and simmer for another 10 minutes, or until the fish is cooked through and flaky.

4. **Serve:** Garnish with fresh cilantro and serve with rice or warm bread.

Nutritional information per serving: 320 calories, 30 grams protein, 10 grams fat, 25 grams carbohydrates

Expert TIP: The combination of smoked paprika and cumin gives this stew a warming, spicy kick, perfect for a cozy fall evening.

VEGAN SOUPS

CREAMY VEGAN CORN AND POTATO CHOWDER

Best season: Winter
Gluten-free

Servings

4

Preparation Time

10 minutes

Cooking Time

30 minutes

YOU WILL NEED:

- 1 tablespoon olive oil (15 milliliters)
- 1 small onion, diced
- 2 cloves garlic, minced
- 3 medium potatoes, diced
- 2 cups fresh or frozen corn (300 grams)
- 4 cups vegetable broth (1 liter)
- 1 cup coconut milk (240 milliliters)
- 1 teaspoon smoked paprika
- 1 teaspoon sea salt
- 1/2 teaspoon black pepper
- 2 tablespoons fresh parsley, chopped

METHOD:

1. **Sauté the Aromatics:** Heat olive oil in a large pot over medium heat. Add diced onion and garlic, cooking for 5 minutes until softened.

2. **Simmer Potatoes and Corn:** Stir in the diced potatoes, corn, vegetable broth, smoked paprika, salt, and pepper. Bring to a boil, reduce heat, and simmer for 20 minutes until the potatoes are tender.

3. **Add Coconut Milk:** Stir in the coconut milk and cook for an additional 5 minutes.

4. **Finish and Serve:** Use an immersion blender to purée part of the soup for a creamier texture, leaving some chunks for heartiness. Garnish with fresh parsley.

Nutritional information per serving: 360 calories, 6 grams protein, 18 grams fat, 45 grams carbohydrates

Expert TIP: The coconut milk gives this chowder a creamy, rich consistency without any dairy. Add a dash of cayenne for a spicy kick!

SMOKY CHICKPEA AND SPINACH STEW

Best season: Winter
Gluten-free

Servings

4

Preparation Time

10 minutes

Cooking Time

30 minutes

YOU WILL NEED:

- 1 tablespoon olive oil (15 milliliters)
- 1 small onion, diced
- 2 cloves garlic, minced
- 1 can chickpeas, drained and rinsed (400 grams)
- 1 can diced tomatoes (400 grams)
- 4 cups vegetable broth (1 liter)
- 1 teaspoon smoked paprika
- 1 teaspoon ground cumin
- 1/2 teaspoon sea salt
- 1/4 teaspoon black pepper
- 2 cups fresh spinach leaves (120 grams)

METHOD:

1. **Cook Aromatics:** Heat olive oil in a large pot over medium heat. Add the onion and garlic, cooking for 5 minutes until softened.

2. **Simmer Chickpeas and Tomatoes:** Stir in chickpeas, diced tomatoes, vegetable broth, smoked paprika, cumin, salt, and pepper. Bring to a boil, reduce heat, and simmer for 20 minutes.

3. **Add Spinach:** Stir in the fresh spinach and cook for another 5 minutes until wilted.

4. **Serve:** Serve warm with a squeeze of lemon juice for added brightness.

Nutritional information per serving: 310 calories, 14 grams protein, 8 grams fat, 45 grams carbohydrates

Expert TIP: The smoked paprika gives the stew a deep, rich flavor, mimicking a slow-cooked, smoky effect. Pair it with quinoa or brown rice for a complete meal.

SPICY BLACK BEAN AND QUINOA STEW

Best season: Winter
Gluten-free, High-protein

Servings

4

Preparation Time

10 minutes

Cooking Time

35 minutes

YOU WILL NEED:

- 1 tablespoon olive oil (15 milliliters)
- 1 small onion, chopped
- 2 cloves garlic, minced
- 1 teaspoon ground cumin
- 1 teaspoon smoked paprika
- 1/2 teaspoon chili powder
- 1 cup quinoa (200 grams)
- 1 can black beans, drained and rinsed (400 grams)
- 1 can diced tomatoes (400 grams)
- 4 cups vegetable broth (1 liter)
- 1 teaspoon sea salt
- 1/4 teaspoon black pepper
- 1/4 cup fresh cilantro, chopped

METHOD:

1. **Cook Aromatics:** Heat olive oil in a large pot. Add onion and garlic, sautéing for 5 minutes until softened.

2. **Add Spices and Quinoa:** Stir in cumin, smoked paprika, chili powder, and quinoa. Cook for 2 minutes to toast the quinoa and bloom the spices.

3. **Simmer with beans:** Add black beans, diced tomatoes, and vegetable broth. Bring to a boil, reduce heat, and simmer for 25-30 minutes until the quinoa is cooked through.

4. **Serve:** Garnish with fresh cilantro and serve hot with lime wedges on the side.

Nutritional information per serving: 390 calories, 16 grams protein, 10 grams fat, 60 grams carbohydrates

Expert TIP: For added texture, you can top this stew with sliced avocado or tortilla strips for a crunchy finish.

BUTTERNUT SQUASH AND APPLE SOUP

Best season: Fall
Gluten-free, Dairy-free

Servings

4

Preparation Time

10 minutes

Cooking Time

30 minutes

YOU WILL NEED:

- 1 tablespoon coconut oil (15 milliliters)
- 1 medium butternut squash, peeled and cubed
- 2 medium apples, peeled and chopped
- 1 small onion, diced
- 4 cups vegetable broth (1 liter)
- 1 teaspoon ground cinnamon
- 1/2 teaspoon ground nutmeg
- 1 teaspoon sea salt
- 1/2 teaspoon black pepper
- 1/2 cup coconut milk (120 milliliters)

METHOD:

1. **Sauté Vegetables and Fruit:** Heat coconut oil in a large pot. Add butternut squash, apples, and onion, cooking for 5-7 minutes until softened.

2. **Simmer the Soup:** Pour in the vegetable broth, cinnamon, nutmeg, salt, and pepper. Bring to a boil, reduce heat, and simmer for 20 minutes until the squash is tender.

3. **Purée and Add Coconut Milk:** Use an immersion blender to purée the soup until smooth. Stir in coconut milk and adjust seasoning.

4. **Serve:** Serve warm with a drizzle of extra coconut milk on top for added creaminess.

Nutritional information per serving: 340 calories, 4 grams protein 12 grams fat, 55 grams carbohydrates

Expert TIP: The natural sweetness of the apples perfectly complements the richness of the squash, making this a cozy fall favorite.

CURRIED CAULIFLOWER AND RED LENTIL SOUP

Best season: Winter
Gluten-free, Dairy-free

Servings

Preparation Time

Cooking Time

4   **10 minutes**   **30 minutes**

YOU WILL NEED:

- 1 tablespoon olive oil (15 milliliters)
- 1 small onion, diced
- 2 cloves garlic, minced
- 1 tablespoon curry powder
- 1 teaspoon ground turmeric
- 1 small cauliflower, cut into florets
- 1 cup red lentils (200 grams)
- 4 cups vegetable broth (1 liter)
- 1 teaspoon sea salt
- 1/2 teaspoon black pepper
- 1/4 cup fresh cilantro, chopped

METHOD:

1. **Sauté the Onion:** Heat olive oil in a large pot. Add the onion and garlic, cooking for 5 minutes until softened.
2. **Add Spices and Cauliflower:** Stir in the curry powder and turmeric. Add the cauliflower florets and stir to coat with the spices.
3. **Simmer with Lentils:** Add red lentils, vegetable broth, salt, and pepper. Bring to a boil, reduce heat, and simmer for 20 minutes until the lentils are tender.
4. **Finish and Serve:** Garnish with fresh cilantro and serve hot with naan or crusty bread.

Nutritional information per serving: 370 calories, 18 grams protein, 8 grams fat, 55 grams carbohydrates

Expert TIP: The curry powder adds warmth and depth, while the red lentils create a rich, creamy texture without any added cream.

HEARTY KIDNEY BEAN AND SWEET POTATO STEW

Best season: Winter
Gluten-free, Dairy-free

Servings

Preparation Time

Cooking Time

4   **15 minutes**   **40 minutes**

YOU WILL NEED:

- 2 tablespoons olive oil (30 milliliters)
- 1 small onion, diced
- 2 cloves garlic, minced
- 2 medium sweet potatoes, peeled and cubed
- 1 can kidney beans, drained and rinsed (400 grams)
- 1 can diced tomatoes (400 grams)
- 4 cups vegetable broth (1 liter)
- 1 teaspoon ground cumin
- 1 teaspoon smoked paprika
- 1/2 teaspoon ground coriander
- 1 teaspoon sea salt
- 1/4 teaspoon black pepper
- 1 cup kale or spinach, chopped
- 1 tablespoon fresh cilantro, chopped
- 1 tablespoon lime juice

METHOD:

1. **Sauté Aromatics:** Heat olive oil in a large pot over medium heat. Add the diced onion and garlic, cooking for about 5 minutes until softened.

2. **Add Sweet Potatoes and Spices:** Stir in the cubed sweet potatoes, cumin, smoked paprika, coriander, salt, and pepper. Cook for 2-3 minutes to coat the sweet potatoes with the spices.

3. **Simmer with Tomatoes and Beans:** Add the kidney beans, diced tomatoes, and vegetable broth. Bring the stew to a boil, reduce heat, and simmer for 25-30 minutes, or until the sweet potatoes are tender.

4. **Add Greens and Finish:** Stir in the chopped kale or spinach and cook for another 5 minutes until wilted.

5. **Serve:** Garnish with fresh cilantro and a squeeze of lime juice for brightness.

Nutritional information per serving: 350 calories, 14 grams protein, 10 grams fat, 55 grams carbohydrates

Expert TIP: The combination of kidney beans and sweet potatoes makes this stew hearty and filling, while the smoked paprika adds a subtle warmth. For extra texture, you can top it with avocado slices or tortilla chips.

HEARTY VEGETABLE AND FARRO STEW

Best season: Winter
Gluten-free option (with quinoa instead of farro)

Servings	Preparation Time	Cooking Time
4	15 minutes	40 minutes

YOU WILL NEED:

- 2 tablespoons olive oil (30 milliliters)
- 1 small onion, diced
- 2 cloves garlic, minced
- 1 large carrot, sliced
- 1 zucchini, diced
- 1/2 cup farro (100 grams)
- 1 can diced tomatoes (400 grams)
- 4 cups vegetable broth (1 liter)
- 1 teaspoon dried thyme
- 1 teaspoon dried basil
- 1/2 teaspoon sea salt
- 1/4 teaspoon black pepper
- 2 cups chopped kale (120 grams)

METHOD:

1. **Sauté Vegetables:** Heat olive oil in a large pot over medium heat. Add onion, garlic, and carrots. Cook for 5 minutes until softened.

2. **Add Grains and Broth:** Stir in the farro, diced tomatoes, vegetable broth, thyme, basil, salt, and pepper. Bring to a boil, then reduce heat and simmer for 25 minutes.

3. **Add Zucchini and Kale:** Add the diced zucchini and chopped kale. Simmer for another 10 minutes until the farro is tender.

4. **Serve:** Ladle into bowls and enjoy with a sprinkle of fresh herbs or a squeeze of lemon juice.

Nutritional information per serving: 390 calories, 14 grams protein, 12 grams fat, 50 grams carbohydrates

Expert TIP: Farro adds a chewy texture and nutty flavor, making this stew hearty and satisfying. Substitute with quinoa for a gluten-free option.

COCONUT AND RED LENTIL CHOWDER

Best season: Fall/Winter
Gluten-free

Servings	Preparation Time	Cooking Time
4	10 minutes	30 minutes

YOU WILL NEED:

- 1 tablespoon coconut oil (15 milliliters)
- 1 small onion, diced
- 2 cloves garlic, minced
- 1 tablespoon fresh ginger, grated
- 1 cup red lentils (200 grams)
- 1 can coconut milk (400 milliliters)
- 4 cups vegetable broth (1 liter)
- 1 teaspoon curry powder
- 1/2 teaspoon ground cumin
- 1/2 teaspoon sea salt
- 1/4 teaspoon black pepper
- 1 tablespoon lime juice
- 2 tablespoons fresh cilantro, chopped

METHOD:

1. **Sauté the Aromatics:** Heat coconut oil in a large pot. Add onion, garlic, and ginger, cooking for 5 minutes.

2. **Add Lentils and Spices:** Stir in red lentils, curry powder, cumin, salt, and pepper. Cook for 2 minutes to toast the spices.

3. **Simmer with Coconut Milk:** Add vegetable broth and coconut milk. Bring to a boil, then reduce heat and simmer for 20 minutes until the lentils are tender.

4. **Finish and Serve:** Stir in lime juice and garnish with fresh cilantro. Serve with naan or over rice.

Nutritional information per serving: 420 calories, 18 grams protein, 16 grams fat, 50 grams carbohydrates

Expert TIP: The combination of red lentils and coconut milk creates a creamy, rich chowder, with warming spices like curry adding depth.

FRENCH-INSPIRED MUSHROOM AND LEEK CHOWDER

Best season: Winter
Gluten-free

Servings Preparation Time Cooking Time

4 **15 minutes** **30 minutes**

YOU WILL NEED:

- 2 tablespoons olive oil (30 milliliters)
- 1 small onion, diced
- 2 leeks, white and light green parts only, thinly sliced
- 3 cloves garlic, minced
- 10 ounces cremini mushrooms, sliced (300 grams)
- 3 medium potatoes, peeled and diced
- 4 cups vegetable broth (1 liter)
- 1 cup unsweetened almond milk (240 milliliters)
- 1 teaspoon dried thyme
- 1 teaspoon sea salt
- 1/2 teaspoon black pepper
- 1 tablespoon fresh parsley, chopped

METHOD:

1. **Sauté the Vegetables:** Heat olive oil in a large pot over medium heat. Add onion, leeks, and garlic, cooking for 5 minutes until softened.

2. **Cook the Mushrooms:** Stir in the sliced mushrooms and cook for 5-7 minutes until they release their moisture and begin to brown.

3. **Simmer with Potatoes:** Add diced potatoes, vegetable broth, thyme, salt, and pepper. Bring to a boil, reduce heat, and simmer for 20 minutes until the potatoes are tender.

4. **Finish with Almond Milk:** Stir in almond milk and cook for an additional 5 minutes. Adjust seasoning if necessary.

5. **Serve:** Garnish with fresh parsley and serve hot.

Nutritional information per serving: 350 calories, 8 grams protein, 12 grams fat, 45 grams carbohydrates

Expert TIP: The combination of leeks and mushrooms adds a delicate, earthy flavor to this creamy chowder, perfect for a cozy winter meal.

CREAMY BROCCOLI AND WHITE BEAN SOUP

Best season: Winter
Gluten-free

Servings	Preparation Time	Cooking Time
4	10 minutes	25 minutes

YOU WILL NEED:

- 1 tablespoon olive oil (15 milliliters)
- 1 small onion, diced
- 3 cloves garlic, minced
- 4 cups broccoli florets (about 300 grams)
- 1 can white beans, drained and rinsed (400 grams)
- 4 cups vegetable broth (1 liter)
- 1/2 cup coconut milk (120 milliliters)
- 1 teaspoon dried thyme
- 1/2 teaspoon sea salt
- 1/2 teaspoon black pepper
- 2 tablespoons nutritional yeast

METHOD:

1. **Sauté the Aromatics:** Heat olive oil in a large pot. Add onion and garlic, cooking for 5 minutes until softened.

2. **Simmer Broccoli and Beans:** Add broccoli, white beans, vegetable broth, thyme, salt, and pepper. Bring to a boil, then reduce heat and simmer for 15 minutes.

3. **Blend and Finish:** Use an immersion blender to purée the soup until smooth. Stir in coconut milk and nutritional yeast, then simmer for another 5 minutes.

4. **Serve:** Garnish with extra broccoli florets or a drizzle of olive oil.

Nutritional information per serving: 340 calories, 10 grams protein, 14 grams fat, 35 grams carbohydrates

Expert TIP: The beans make the soup creamy and protein-packed without the need for dairy. Add a pinch of chili flakes for heat.

CREAMY MUSHROOM AND WILD RICE SOUP

Best season: Winter
Gluten-free

Servings	Preparation Time	Cooking Time
4	10 minutes	45 minutes

YOU WILL NEED:

- 1 tablespoon olive oil (15 milliliters)
- 1 small onion, diced
- 3 cloves garlic, minced
- 10 ounces cremini mushrooms, sliced (300 grams)
- 1/2 cup wild rice (100 grams)
- 4 cups vegetable broth (1 liter)
- 1/2 cup coconut milk (120 milliliters)
- 1 teaspoon dried thyme
- 1 teaspoon sea salt
- 1/2 teaspoon black pepper
- 1 tablespoon fresh parsley, chopped

METHOD:

1. **Cook the Mushrooms:** Heat olive oil in a large pot over medium heat. Add onion, garlic, and mushrooms. Cook for 8-10 minutes until the mushrooms release their liquid and are golden brown.

2. **Add Rice and Broth:** Stir in wild rice, vegetable broth, thyme, salt, and pepper. Bring to a boil, reduce heat, and simmer for 40 minutes until the rice is tender.

3. **Finish with Coconut Milk:** Stir in coconut milk and cook for another 5 minutes. Adjust seasoning to taste.

4. **Serve:** Garnish with fresh parsley and serve hot with crusty bread.

Nutritional information per serving: 360 calories, 10 grams protein, 16 grams fat, 40 grams carbohydrates

Expert TIP: The earthy flavor of wild rice complements the mushrooms, while coconut milk gives the soup a creamy finish without dairy.

VEGAN FRENCH ONION SOUP

Best season: Winter
Gluten-free option (with gluten-free bread)

Servings	Preparation Time	Cooking Time
4	15 minutes	1 hour

YOU WILL NEED:

- 2 tablespoons olive oil (30 milliliters)
- 4 large yellow onions, thinly sliced
- 4 cloves garlic, minced
- 1 tablespoon balsamic vinegar
- 1 tablespoon soy sauce or tamari (for gluten-free option)
- 6 cups vegetable broth (1.5 liters)
- 1/2 cup dry white wine (120 milliliters, optional)
- 2 teaspoons fresh thyme leaves or 1 teaspoon dried thyme
- 1 bay leaf
- 1/2 teaspoon sea salt
- 1/4 teaspoon black pepper
- 4 slices baguette or crusty bread (use gluten-free bread for GF option)
- 1 cup vegan shredded cheese (such as vegan mozzarella or Gruyère style)

METHOD:

1. **Caramelize the Onions:** Heat olive oil in a large pot over medium heat. Add the sliced onions and cook for 20-30 minutes, stirring often, until they are golden brown and caramelized. If the onions start to stick, add a splash of water to prevent burning.

2. **Add Garlic and Deglaze:** Stir in the minced garlic, cooking for another minute. Deglaze the pot by adding balsamic vinegar and soy sauce, scraping up any browned bits from the bottom of the pot.

3. **Simmer the Soup:** Add vegetable broth, white wine (if using), thyme, bay leaf, salt, and pepper. Bring to a boil, then reduce heat and simmer for 20 minutes, allowing the flavors to meld.

4. **Toast the Bread:** While the soup simmers, toast the bread slices in a toaster or oven until they are golden and crispy.

5. **Assemble and Serve:** Ladle the soup into oven-safe bowls, place a slice of toasted bread on top of each bowl, and sprinkle with vegan cheese. Broil in the oven for 2-3 minutes, or until the cheese is melted and bubbly.

6. **Serve:** Remove the bay leaf, garnish with extra thyme, and serve hot.

Nutritional information per serving: 320 calories, 8 grams protein, 12 grams fat, 40 grams carbohydrates

Expert TIP: The slow caramelization of the onions gives this soup its signature rich flavor. The vegan cheese and soy sauce provide depth, mimicking the umami of the original dish. For an even heartier version, serve with extra crusty bread on the side.

Best season: Winter
Gluten-free, Dairy-free

Servings
4

Preparation Time
15 minutes

Cooking Time
30 minutes

YOU WILL NEED:

- 1 tablespoon olive oil (15 milliliters)
- 1 small onion, diced
- 4 large carrots, peeled and chopped
- 2 cloves garlic, minced
- 1 tablespoon fresh ginger, grated
- 1 teaspoon ground coriander
- Zest of 1 orange
- Juice of 2 oranges
- 4 cups vegetable broth (1 liter)
- 1/2 teaspoon sea salt
- 1/4 teaspoon black pepper
- 2 tablespoons tahini
- 1 tablespoon fresh parsley, chopped

METHOD:

1. **Sauté the Vegetables:** Heat olive oil in a large pot over medium heat. Add the diced onion, garlic, and chopped carrots, cooking for 5-7 minutes until softened.

2. **Add Ginger and Spices:** Stir in the grated ginger, ground coriander, and orange zest, cooking for another minute to release the flavors.

3. **Simmer with Orange Juice:** Pour in the orange juice and vegetable broth. Bring to a boil, reduce heat, and simmer for 20 minutes until the carrots are tender.

4. **Blend and Swirl:** Use an immersion blender to purée the soup until smooth. Season with sea salt and pepper.

5. **Serve:** Ladle the soup into bowls and drizzle with tahini. Garnish with fresh parsley for a burst of color.

Nutritional information per serving: 320 calories, 6 grams protein, 14 grams fat, 42 grams carbohydrates

Expert TIP: The fresh orange juice adds a bright citrusy twist to this creamy carrot soup, while the tahini gives it a rich and nutty finish. Try adding roasted chickpeas for extra crunch!

SMOKY EGGPLANT AND BLACK LENTIL STEW

Best season: Winter
Gluten-free, Dairy-free

Servings

4

Preparation Time

20 minutes

Cooking Time

45 minutes

YOU WILL NEED:

- 2 tablespoons olive oil (30 milliliters)
- 1 large eggplant, cubed
- 1 small onion, diced
- 3 cloves garlic, minced
- 1 teaspoon smoked paprika
- 1 teaspoon ground cumin
- 1 cup dried black lentils (200 grams)
- 1 can diced tomatoes (400 grams)
- 4 cups vegetable broth (1 liter)
- 1 teaspoon sea salt
- 1/4 teaspoon black pepper
- 2 tablespoons fresh mint, chopped
- 1 tablespoon lemon juice

METHOD:

1. **Sauté Eggplant and Onion:** Heat olive oil in a large pot over medium heat. Add cubed eggplant and diced onion, cooking for 10 minutes until the eggplant becomes soft and browned.

2. **Add Garlic and Spices:** Stir in garlic, smoked paprika, and cumin, cooking for another 2 minutes to release the aroma of the spices.

3. **Simmer with Lentils and Tomatoes:** Add the black lentils, diced tomatoes, and vegetable broth. Bring to a boil, reduce heat, and simmer for 30 minutes until the lentils are tender.

4. **Finish with Lemon Juice:** Stir in the lemon juice and adjust seasoning with salt and pepper.

5. **Serve:** Garnish with fresh mint and serve hot with flatbread or rice.

Nutritional information per serving: 390 calories, 18 grams protein, 14 grams fat, 50 grams carbohydrates

Expert TIP: The smoky flavor of the paprika complements the roasted eggplant, creating a deep and robust stew. The mint and lemon juice add freshness, balancing the earthy lentils.

MEXICAN BLACK BEAN AND SWEET CORN CHILI

Best season: Fall
Gluten-free

Servings

4

Preparation Time

15 minutes

Cooking Time

40 minutes

YOU WILL NEED:

- 1 tablespoon olive oil (15 milliliters)
- 1 small onion, diced
- 3 cloves garlic, minced
- 1 red bell pepper, diced
- 1 can black beans, drained and rinsed (400 grams)
- 2 cups fresh or frozen corn (300 grams)
- 1 can diced tomatoes (400 grams)
- 1 tablespoon chili powder
- 1 teaspoon ground cumin
- 1 teaspoon smoked paprika
- 1 teaspoon sea salt
- 1/2 teaspoon black pepper
- 1/2 teaspoon cayenne pepper (optional for heat)
- 4 cups vegetable broth (1 liter)
- 1/4 cup fresh cilantro, chopped

METHOD:

1. **Sauté the Vegetables:** Heat olive oil in a large pot. Add the onion, garlic, and bell pepper, cooking for 5 minutes until softened.

2. **Add Spices:** Stir in the chili powder, cumin, smoked paprika, salt, pepper, and cayenne (if using). Cook for another minute to toast the spices.

3. **Simmer with Beans and Corn:** Add black beans, corn, diced tomatoes, and vegetable broth. Bring to a boil, reduce heat, and simmer for 25-30 minutes.

4. **Serve:** Garnish with fresh cilantro and serve with avocado slices and lime wedges.

Nutritional information per serving: 380 calories, 15 grams protein, 9 grams fat, 60 grams carbohydrates

Expert TIP: This chili has a smoky flavor, thanks to the smoked paprika, and pairs perfectly with tortilla chips or cornbread.

SPICY LENTIL AND KALE STEW

Best season: Winter
Gluten-free, High-protein

Servings

4

Preparation Time

10 minutes

Cooking Time

40 minutes

YOU WILL NEED:

- 1 tablespoon olive oil (15 milliliters)
- 1 small onion, diced
- 2 cloves garlic, minced
- 1 cup dried green lentils (200 grams)
- 4 cups vegetable broth (1 liter)
- 1 can diced tomatoes (400 grams)
- 1 teaspoon smoked paprika
- 1 teaspoon ground cumin
- 1/2 teaspoon chili powder
- 2 cups chopped kale (120 grams)
- 1 teaspoon sea salt
- 1/4 teaspoon black pepper

METHOD:

1. **Cook the Aromatics:** Heat olive oil in a large pot. Add onion and garlic, cooking for 5 minutes.

2. **Add Lentils and Spices:** Stir in lentils, vegetable broth, diced tomatoes, smoked paprika, cumin, and chili powder. Bring to a boil, reduce heat, and simmer for 30 minutes.

3. **Add Kale:** Stir in chopped kale, salt, and pepper. Simmer for another 10 minutes until the kale is wilted and the lentils are tender.

4. **Serve:** Garnish with fresh cilantro or a squeeze of lime.

Nutritional information per serving: 390 calories, 18 grams protein, 10 grams fat, 60 grams carbohydrates

Expert TIP: The combination of lentils and kale creates a nutrient-packed stew with plenty of fiber and protein, perfect for a filling dinner.

TOMATO AND ROASTED RED PEPPER BISQUE

Best season: Winter
Gluten-free

Servings

Preparation Time

Cooking Time

4   10 minutes   35 minutes

YOU WILL NEED:

- 1 tablespoon olive oil (15 milliliters)
- 1 small onion, diced
- 3 cloves garlic, minced
- 1 can diced tomatoes (400 grams)
- 2 large roasted red peppers, chopped
- 4 cups vegetable broth (1 liter)
- 1 teaspoon dried basil
- 1 teaspoon sea salt
- 1/2 teaspoon black pepper
- 1/2 cup coconut cream (120 milliliters)

METHOD:

1. **Sauté the Aromatics:** Heat olive oil in a large pot. Add onion and garlic, cooking for 5 minutes.

2. **Simmer Tomatoes and Peppers:** Stir in the diced tomatoes, roasted red peppers, vegetable broth, basil, salt, and pepper. Bring to a boil, reduce heat, and simmer for 25 minutes.

3. **Purée and Add Coconut Cream:** Blend the soup with an immersion blender until smooth. Stir in coconut cream and adjust seasoning.

4. **Serve:** Serve hot with fresh basil or a drizzle of olive oil.

Nutritional information per serving: 300 calories, 5 grams protein, 14 grams fat, 35 grams carbohydrates

Expert TIP: The roasted red peppers add a smoky depth to the classic tomato bisque. Serve with a vegan grilled cheese for a complete meal.

Best season: Winter
Gluten-free

Servings

4

Preparation Time

15 minutes
(plus 30 minutes soaking time for cashews)

Cooking Time

30 minutes

YOU WILL NEED:

- 1 tablespoon olive oil (15 milliliters)
- 1 small onion, diced
- 3 cloves garlic, minced
- 1 can diced tomatoes (400 grams)
- 4 large fresh tomatoes, chopped
- 1 cup raw cashews, soaked for 30 minutes (150 grams)
- 3 cups vegetable broth (750 milliliters)
- 1 tablespoon tomato paste
- 1 teaspoon smoked paprika
- 1 teaspoon dried basil
- 1 teaspoon sea salt
- 1/2 teaspoon black pepper
- 1/2 cup unsweetened almond milk (120 milliliters)
- 2 tablespoons fresh basil, chopped

METHOD:

1. **Sauté Aromatics:** Heat olive oil in a large pot over medium heat. Add diced onion and garlic, cooking for about 5 minutes until softened.

2. **Add Tomatoes:** Stir in the diced tomatoes (both canned and fresh), tomato paste, smoked paprika, dried basil, salt, and pepper. Cook for 5-7 minutes, allowing the flavors to meld.

3. **Simmer with Broth:** Add the vegetable broth and bring to a boil. Reduce heat and simmer for 20 minutes.

4. **Blend Cashews:** While the soup is simmering, drain the soaked cashews and blend them with almond milk until smooth and creamy.

5. **Combine and Blend:** Add the cashew mixture to the soup. Use an immersion blender to purée the entire mixture until smooth and creamy. Adjust seasoning if needed.

6. **Serve:** Garnish with freshly chopped basil and serve hot, with crusty bread or crackers.

Nutritional information per serving: 420 calories, 12 grams protein, 22 grams fat, 40 grams carbohydrates

Expert TIP: The soaked cashews add a creamy richness to this bisque, giving it a velvety texture without any dairy. For extra depth, roast the fresh tomatoes before adding them to the soup.

Best season: Winter
Gluten-free

Servings	Preparation Time	Cooking Time
4	15 minutes	30 minutes

YOU WILL NEED:

- 2 tablespoons olive oil (30 milliliters)
- 1 small onion, diced
- 2 cloves garlic, minced
- 3 large carrots, peeled and diced
- 2 cups fresh or frozen corn kernels (300 grams)
- 3 medium potatoes, peeled and diced
- 4 cups vegetable broth (1 liter)
- 1 cup coconut milk (240 milliliters)
- 1 teaspoon smoked paprika
- 1 teaspoon sea salt
- 1/2 teaspoon black pepper
- 2 tablespoons fresh parsley, chopped

METHOD:

1. **Sauté the Aromatics:** Heat olive oil in a large pot over medium heat. Add diced onion and garlic, cooking for about 5 minutes until softened.

2. **Simmer Vegetables:** Stir in diced carrots, corn, and potatoes. Pour in the vegetable broth and add smoked paprika, salt, and pepper. Bring to a boil, reduce heat, and simmer for 20 minutes until the potatoes and carrots are tender.

3. **Add Coconut Milk:** Stir in the coconut milk and cook for an additional 5 minutes.

4. **Blend for Creaminess:** Use an immersion blender to purée part of the chowder, leaving some chunks for texture.

5. **Serve:** Garnish with fresh parsley and serve hot, with crusty bread or crackers on the side.

Nutritional information per serving: 390 calories, 7 grams protein 15 grams fat, 52 grams carbohydrates

Expert TIP: The sweetness of the corn and carrots pairs beautifully with the richness of coconut milk. For an extra kick, sprinkle some cayenne pepper or red chili flakes.

AVOCADO AND CUCUMBER GAZPACHO

Servings	Preparation Time	Cooking Time
6	10 minutes	40 minutes

METHOD:

1. Sauté onion and ginger in olive oil until soft.

2. Add pumpkin puree and vegetable stock, simmer for 30 minutes. Season and garnish with pumpkin seeds.

YOU WILL NEED:

- 2 tablespoons olive oil
- 1 onion, diced
- 4 cups pumpkin puree
- 1 tablespoon grated ginger
- 5 cups vegetable stock
- Salt and pepper to taste
- Pumpkin seeds for garnish

SPECIAL OCCASION SOUPS

THANKSGIVING – BUTTERNUT SQUASH AND CHESTNUT SOUP

Best season: Fall
Holiday: Thanksgiving
(Fourth Thursday in November)
Gluten-free, Dairy-free

Servings

6

Preparation Time

20 minutes

Cooking Time

45 minutes

YOU WILL NEED:

- 2 tablespoons olive oil (30 milliliters)
- 1 medium butternut squash, peeled and cubed
- 1 small onion, diced
- 2 cloves garlic, minced
- 1 cup cooked and peeled chestnuts (150 grams)
- 4 cups vegetable broth (1 liter)
- 1 teaspoon ground cinnamon
- 1/2 teaspoon ground nutmeg
- 1 teaspoon sea salt
- 1/2 teaspoon black pepper
- 1/2 cup coconut milk (120 milliliters)
- 2 tablespoons fresh sage, chopped

METHOD:

1. **Sauté Vegetables:** Heat olive oil in a large pot. Add the diced onion, garlic, and cubed butternut squash, cooking for 10 minutes until softened.

2. **Simmer with Chestnuts:** Add the chestnuts, vegetable broth, cinnamon, nutmeg, salt, and pepper. Simmer for 30 minutes until the squash is tender.

3. **Purée and Add Coconut Milk:** Use an immersion blender to purée the soup until smooth. Stir in coconut milk and fresh sage.

4. **Serve:** Garnish with extra fresh sage and serve with warm crusty bread.

Nutritional information per serving: 340 calories, 6 grams protein, 14 grams fat, 50 grams carbohydrates

Expert TIP: Chestnuts add a rich, earthy flavor to this elegant soup, making it a perfect starter for Thanksgiving dinner.

SPRING FESTIVAL – SPICED YELLOW LENTIL SOUP

Best season: Spring
Holiday: Spring Festival
Gluten-free, Dairy-free

Servings

4

Preparation Time

15 minutes

Cooking Time

30 minutes

METHOD:

1. **Sauté Vegetables:** Heat olive oil in a pot. Add onion, garlic, carrot, and zucchini, sautéing for 5 minutes.

2. **Simmer:** Add vegetable broth, tomatoes, dried basil, salt, and pepper. Bring to a boil, then reduce heat and simmer for 20 minutes.

3. **Add Pasta and Greens:** Stir in the pasta and cook for 10 minutes. Add spinach just before serving.

4. **Serve:** Garnish with fresh basil and serve with crusty bread.

YOU WILL NEED:

- 2 tablespoons olive oil (30 milliliters)
- 1 small onion, diced
- 2 cloves garlic, minced
- 1 carrot, sliced
- 1 zucchini, chopped
- 1/2 cup green peas (80 grams)
- 4 cups vegetable broth (1 liter)
- 1/2 cup small pasta (100 grams, gluten-free if needed)
- 1 can diced tomatoes (400 grams)
- 1 teaspoon dried basil
- 1 teaspoon sea salt
- 1/4 teaspoon black pepper
- 2 cups fresh spinach, chopped (120 grams)
- 2 tablespoons fresh basil, chopped

Nutritional information per serving: 320 calories, 10 grams protein, 8 grams fat, 52 grams carbohydrates

Expert TIP: This light and fresh minestrone is perfect for celebrating the arrival of spring during Easter.

VALENTINE'S DAY – CREAMY VEGAN TOMATO AND BASIL BISQUE

Best season: Winter
Holiday: Valentine's Day (February 14)

Servings	Preparation Time	Cooking Time
4	15 minutes	30 minutes

YOU WILL NEED:

- 2 tablespoons olive oil (30 milliliters)
- 1 small onion, diced
- 4 cloves garlic, minced
- 1 can diced tomatoes (400 grams)
- 4 large ripe tomatoes, chopped
- 4 cups vegetable broth (1 liter)
- 1 teaspoon sugar
- 1/2 teaspoon sea salt
- 1/4 teaspoon black pepper
- 1/2 cup coconut cream (120 milliliters)
- 1/4 cup fresh basil, chopped
- 1 tablespoon balsamic vinegar (optional)

METHOD:

1. **Sauté Aromatics:** Heat olive oil in a large pot. Add diced onion and garlic, cooking for 5 minutes until softened.

2. **Simmer Tomatoes:** Add diced tomatoes (both canned and fresh), vegetable broth, sugar, salt, and pepper. Bring to a boil, reduce heat, and simmer for 20 minutes.

3. **Blend and Add Coconut Cream:** Use an immersion blender to purée the soup until smooth. Stir in the coconut cream and balsamic vinegar for richness.

4. **Serve:** Garnish with fresh basil and serve with crusty bread or vegan grilled cheese for a romantic dinner.

Nutritional information per serving: 320 calories, 6 grams protein, 16 grams fat, 38 grams carbohydrates

Expert TIP: The creamy, silky texture of this tomato bisque is perfect for a cozy Valentine's dinner. Pair with a glass of wine for a special touch!

Best season: Summer
Holiday: Labor Day (First Monday in September)
Gluten-free, Dairy-free

Servings	Preparation Time	Cooking Time
4	**15 minutes**	**30 minutes**

YOU WILL NEED:

- 2 tablespoons olive oil (30 milliliters)
- 1 small onion, diced
- 2 cloves garlic, minced
- 4 ears fresh corn, grilled and kernels removed
- 1 can black beans, drained and rinsed (400 grams)
- 2 medium potatoes, peeled and diced
- 4 cups vegetable broth (1 liter)
- 1 teaspoon smoked paprika
- 1 teaspoon ground cumin
- 1 teaspoon sea salt
- 1/4 teaspoon black pepper
- 1/2 cup coconut milk (120 milliliters)
- 2 tablespoons fresh cilantro, chopped

METHOD:

1. **Sauté Aromatics:** Heat olive oil in a large pot. Add the diced onion and garlic, cooking for 5 minutes until softened.

2. **Simmer Potatoes and Corn:** Add grilled corn kernels, diced potatoes, vegetable broth, smoked paprika, cumin, salt, and pepper. Bring to a boil, reduce heat, and simmer for 20 minutes.

3. **Add Black Beans and Coconut Milk:** Stir in the black beans and coconut milk, simmering for another 5 minutes.

4. **Serve:** Garnish with fresh cilantro and serve with grilled bread or tortilla chips.

Nutritional information per serving: 380 calories, 10 grams protein, 16 grams fat, 55 grams carbohydrates

Expert TIP: The smoky grilled corn and rich coconut milk make this chowder perfect for a Labor Day BBQ. You can prepare the corn on the grill for extra summer flavor.

Best season: Summer
Holiday: Summer Festivities
Gluten-free, Dairy-free

Servings
4

Preparation Time
15 minutes

Cooking Time
25 minutes

YOU WILL NEED:

- 2 tablespoons olive oil (30 milliliters)
- 1 small onion, diced
- 2 cloves garlic, minced
- 4 ears fresh corn, kernels removed (or 2 cups frozen corn)
- 2 medium zucchinis, chopped
- 4 cups vegetable broth (1 liter)
- 1 cup coconut milk (240 milliliters)
- 1 teaspoon smoked paprika
- 1/2 teaspoon ground cumin
- 1 teaspoon sea salt
- 1/4 teaspoon black pepper
- 2 tablespoons fresh parsley, chopped

METHOD:

1. **Sauté Vegetables:** Heat olive oil in a large pot. Add onion and garlic, cooking for 5 minutes.
2. **Simmer with Corn and Zucchini:** Stir in the corn, zucchini, vegetable broth, smoked paprika, cumin, salt, and pepper. Bring to a boil, reduce heat, and simmer for 15 minutes.
3. **Add Coconut Milk:** Stir in the coconut milk and cook for another 5 minutes.
4. **Serve:** Garnish with fresh parsley and serve with crusty bread.

Nutritional information per serving: 320 calories, 7 grams protein, 14 grams fat, 42 grams carbohydrates

Expert TIP: The sweetness of the corn pairs beautifully with the creamy coconut milk, making it perfect for summer gatherings.

Best season: Summer
Holiday: Fourth of July (July 4)
Gluten-free, Dairy-free

Servings	Preparation Time	Cooking Time

4	15 minutes	1 hour

YOU WILL NEED:

- 4 cups watermelon, cubed (600 grams)
- 3 large ripe tomatoes, chopped
- 1 small cucumber, peeled and diced
- 1 small red bell pepper, chopped
- 1/4 cup red onion, finely chopped
- 1 clove garlic, minced
- 1 tablespoon red wine vinegar
- 2 tablespoons olive oil (30 milliliters)
- 1/2 teaspoon sea salt
- 1/4 teaspoon black pepper
- 1/4 cup fresh basil leaves, chopped
- 1 tablespoon lime juice

METHOD:

1. **Blend the Base:** In a blender or food processor, combine the cubed watermelon, chopped tomatoes, cucumber, red bell pepper, and red onion. Add the minced garlic, red wine vinegar, olive oil, salt, and pepper. Blend until smooth.

2. **Chill the Gazpacho:** Transfer the blended mixture to a large bowl, cover, and refrigerate for at least 1 hour to allow the flavors to meld and the soup to chill thoroughly.

3. **Finish with Fresh Herbs:** Before serving, stir in the fresh basil and lime juice for brightness and extra flavor.

4. **Serve:** Ladle the chilled soup into bowls or glasses. Garnish with extra basil leaves or a drizzle of olive oil for a refreshing touch.

Nutritional information per serving: 180 calories, 4 grams protein, 9 grams fat, 23 grams carbohydrates

Expert TIP: This light, refreshing soup is perfect for a hot Fourth of July celebration, offering a cool contrast to grilled foods. The watermelon adds a natural sweetness, while the tomatoes and basil give it a savory, herby flavor that's ideal for summer.

Best season: Fall
Holiday: Halloween (October 31)
Gluten-free, Dairy-free

Servings

Preparation Time

4   **15 minutes**

YOU WILL NEED:

- 2 tablespoons olive oil (30 milliliters)
- 1 small onion, diced
- 2 cloves garlic, minced
- 2 large sweet potatoes, peeled and cubed
- 3 large carrots, peeled and chopped
- 4 cups vegetable broth (1 liter)
- 1 teaspoon ground cinnamon
- 1/2 teaspoon ground nutmeg
- 1 teaspoon sea salt
- 1/4 teaspoon black pepper
- 1/2 cup coconut milk (120 milliliters)
- 1 tablespoon lime juice

FOR THE "SPIDER WEB" GARNISH:

- 1/4 cup vegan sour cream (60 milliliters)
- 1-2 teaspoons water (to thin the sour cream)

METHOD:

1. **Sauté Aromatics:** Heat olive oil in a large pot over medium heat. Add diced onion and garlic, sautéing for about 5 minutes until softened and fragrant.
2. **Cook Vegetables:** Add cubed sweet potatoes, carrots, cinnamon, nutmeg, salt, and pepper. Stir and cook for 2 minutes, allowing the spices to bloom.
3. **Simmer Soup:** Pour in the vegetable broth and bring to a boil. Lower the heat and simmer for 20 minutes, or until the sweet potatoes and carrots are soft and tender.
4. **Blend and Add Coconut Milk:** Use an immersion blender to purée the soup until smooth. Stir in coconut milk and lime juice to add creaminess and balance the flavors.
5. **Create the Spider Web:** In a small bowl, mix the vegan sour cream with a little water to thin it to a pourable consistency. Transfer the mixture to a squeeze bottle or a piping bag with a small tip.
6. **Serve:** Ladle the soup into bowls. Using the sour cream, pipe a spiral starting from the center of each bowl. Then, drag a toothpick from the center outward to create a spider web effect.

Nutritional information per serving: 300 calories, 5 grams protein, 12 grams fat, 45 grams carbohydrates

Expert TIP: The sweet potato and carrot base creates a naturally sweet, creamy soup that pairs perfectly with the warmth of cinnamon and nutmeg. The "spider web" garnish is a fun and spooky addition for Halloween dinner, perfect for family gatherings or parties.

Best season: Winter
Holiday: New Year's Day
Gluten-free, Dairy-free

Servings

4

Preparation Time

15 minutes

Cooking Time

45 minutes

YOU WILL NEED:

- 1 tablespoon olive oil (15 milliliters)
- 1 small onion, diced
- 3 cloves garlic, minced
- 1 cup dried black-eyed peas (or 1 can, drained and rinsed)
- 4 cups vegetable broth (1 liter)
- 2 cups collard greens, chopped (120 grams)
- 1 large sweet potato, peeled and diced
- 1 teaspoon smoked paprika
- 1 teaspoon dried thyme
- 1/2 teaspoon sea salt
- 1/4 teaspoon black pepper
- 1 tablespoon apple cider vinegar

METHOD:

1. **Sauté the Aromatics:** Heat olive oil in a large pot. Add onion and garlic, cooking for 5 minutes until softened.
2. **Simmer with Black-Eyed Peas:** Add the black-eyed peas, vegetable broth, smoked paprika, thyme, salt, and pepper. Simmer for 30 minutes (or 15 if using canned peas).
3. **Add Sweet Potatoes and Greens:** Stir in the diced sweet potatoes and collard greens. Simmer for another 15 minutes until the sweet potatoes are tender.
4. **Finish and Serve:** Stir in apple cider vinegar for brightness. Serve hot with cornbread or over rice.

Nutritional information per serving: 360 calories, 14 grams protein, 8 grams fat, 60 grams carbohydrates

Expert TIP: This traditional New Year's dish symbolizes good luck and prosperity for the year ahead.

CHRISTMAS – MUSHROOM AND BARLEY STEW

Best season: Winter
Holiday: Christmas (December 25)
Gluten-free option (with gluten-free grains)

Servings	Preparation Time	Cooking Time
6	20 minutes	50 minutes

YOU WILL NEED:

- 2 tablespoons olive oil (30 milliliters)
- 1 small onion, diced
- 3 cloves garlic, minced
- 10 ounces cremini mushrooms, sliced (300 grams)
- 1/2 cup pearl barley (100 grams)
- 4 cups vegetable broth (1 liter)
- 1 teaspoon dried thyme
- 1 bay leaf
- 1 teaspoon sea salt
- 1/2 teaspoon black pepper
- 1 cup chopped kale (60 grams)
- 1 tablespoon fresh parsley, chopped

METHOD:

1. **Sauté Aromatics:** Heat olive oil in a large pot. Add the diced onion and garlic, cooking for 5 minutes. Add mushrooms and cook until they release their liquid, about 5 more minutes.

2. **Add Barley and Simmer:** Stir in the barley, vegetable broth, thyme, bay leaf, salt, and pepper. Bring to a boil, reduce heat, and simmer for 40 minutes until the barley is tender.

3. **Add Kale:** Stir in the chopped kale and cook for another 5 minutes until wilted.

4. **Serve:** Garnish with fresh parsley and serve hot with hearty bread.

Nutritional information per serving: 350 calories, 10 grams protein, 12 grams fat, 52 grams carbohydrates

Expert TIP: This rich and earthy stew is perfect for Christmas dinner. The barley gives it a satisfying chew, and the mushrooms add deep umami flavor.

STIRRING IT ALL TOGETHER: A JOURNEY IN EVERY BOWL

As we come to the end of The Soup Cookbook, I want to thank you for joining me on this flavorful journey. My hope is that you've found not just recipes, but inspiration—ways to transform simple ingredients into something extraordinary, and to discover the comfort, joy, and nourishment that a well-crafted bowl of soup can bring to your life.

Throughout this book, we've explored soups for every occasion, season, and dietary need. From hearty winter stews to light summer gazpachos, from rich, creamy bisques to clear, brothy bowls that soothe the soul, the versatility of soup knows no bounds. My goal was to show you that no matter where you are in your cooking journey—whether you're just starting out or you're an experienced home chef—there's always a soup to fit your mood, taste, and lifestyle.

For me, soup has always been about more than just a meal—it's about connection. It connects us to our roots, to the people we share it with, and to the moments of peace and warmth we can find in our busy lives. My wish is that these recipes inspire you to cook more often, to experiment with flavors, and most importantly, to make soup a part of your own story.

Remember, cooking is an evolving journey. You don't need to follow every recipe to the letter—trust your instincts, use what you have, and make each recipe your own. The best soups are those that reflect your creativity and taste, and that bring a sense of comfort to your kitchen.

Thank you for allowing me to be a part of your culinary adventure. I hope these soups bring you as much joy and satisfaction as they have brought me throughout my life. Here's to many more bowls of warmth, flavor, and nourishment—made with love and shared with the ones who matter most.

With heartfelt gratitude,   **Nora J. Shepherd**

Don't miss out on exclusive FREE resources—just scan the QR code to claim them now!

RECIPE INDEX

Made in the USA
Coppell, TX
20 December 2024

43275021R00057